✗

IN THE TRACK OF THE GOSPEL

IN THE TRACK OF THE GOSPEL

*An Outline of the Christian Apostolate
from Pentecost to the Present*

by
ALOYSIUS ROCHE

THE CATHOLIC BOOK CLUB
121 CHARING CROSS ROAD
LONDON, W.C.2

NIHIL OBSTAT: HVBERTVS RICHARDS, S.T.L., L.S.S.
CENSOR DEPVTATVS
IMPRIMATVR: E. MORROGH BERNARD
VICARIVS GENERALIS
WESTMONASTERII: DIE XXVII MARTII MCMLIII

MADE AND PRINTED IN GREAT BRITAIN BY
CHARLES BIRCHALL AND SONS, LTD., LIVERPOOL AND LONDON

PREFACE

THE Master Himself identified the Seed of the Parable with the word of God; the Godspell the Anglo-Saxons called it. And this Seed, carried in all directions by the wind of Pentecost, was destined to produce teeming harvests, many of which are still flourishing, although some have been blighted and have withered away. These, together with the manner of their sowing, this book proposes to trace and to survey after a fashion acceptable to the ordinary or average reader.

A long-drawn-out story it is, to be sure, and an involved one; so that any telling of it, however inadequate, must be accompanied by a formidable accumulation of dates, figures and names, with the consequent risk of slips being made and inaccuracies creeping in. In compiling the major portion of it, the writer had access to no sources other than second-hand ones, the manuals, that is to say, of Church History. These text-books, however, have not always quite the same account to render even of fairly important events; a testimony to the obscurity surrounding missionary enterprises right down to modern times. Not a great deal is known of the persons and processes at work in the conversion of the European continent, certainly not of the eastern and south-eastern parts. As to what was done in the two Americas after their discovery, and in the Far East later on, the sources here are abundant, but they have not yet, or to any great extent, been made available to our part of the world. A recent biography revealed how much we had still to learn, and to unlearn, about so outstanding and so familiar a foreign missionary as St. Francis Xavier.

An endless stream of information now flows in from the mission fields, to well up in the numerous periodicals that are so attractive a feature of the apostolate of our day. But since it is not possible to put into a book more than the book will hold, the writer had no option here but to choose such bits and pieces as seemed to be fair samples of the whole. In these latter days, too, foreign missionary bodies have

multiplied to such a degree that to do anything like justice
to all of them would, of necessity, swell the book to unmanage-
able dimensions.   Here, again, there was no alternative save
the painful one of making a representative selection, presuming
meanwhile upon the spirit of self-effacement and renunciation
animating the absentees.

At the moment, the term Christian Apostolate has, thank
God, a wider connotation than ever before. The contemporary Church is fermenting with projects and organizations - lay and clerical - one and all stemming from Catholic
Action, and one and all claiming the right to a place in the
bag of the Sower who went out to sow his seed. These
movements, though, are important enough to deserve a book
to themselves, and one whose scope is somewhat different
from that of the present work.

The statistics given in the concluding portion of the volume
have been taken from the official Roman publication *Il
Missioni Cattoliche*, the last issue of which appeared in 1950.

It only remains for the author to express a word of thanks
to those who so readily placed their information at his disposal
or allowed him to make use of the materials brought together
in their own books, newspapers and magazines.

CONTENTS

        Explanation of French predominance. Italian Societies.
        German and Dutch enterprises. Society of the Divine
        Word. The Salvatorians. The Benedictines. The
        Franciscans. The Mother of the Africans. Society of St.
        Peter Claver. Father Damien. Work for lepers. Mill
        Hill: Present Statistics. Cardinal Massaia. The Verona
        Fathers. Don Bosco and the Salesians. His missionary
        testament.

XXV.   MISSIONARY SISTERS   160
        Moral necessity of their services. Modern development
        of missionary Sister. Some historical precedents. The
        Dominicans at Martinique. The Ursulines in Quebec.
        Mère Javouhey. Anna Lapini. Hélène Chappotin de
        Neuville and Franciscan Missionaries of Mary. Multi-
        plication of missionary Sisterhoods. Irish nuns in
        Sierra Leone. H'ou-Zah-Mou-Mou. Native nuns. The
        Daughters of Mary. The missionary Sister's vocation.
        The missions placed under the protection of a woman
        saint.

XXVI.   THE CONTEMPORARY SCENE   168
        Advances and set-backs. Pope Pius XI. Vatican
        Exhibition. Catholic Women's Missionary League.
        Mission Sunday. Some statistics. Holland and Switzer-
        land. Canada. U.S.A. and Ireland. Present position in
        China: in Japan: in India: in Africa. Father de
        Foucauld and the conversion of the Arabs. Africa's
        choice. Nationalism in Africa. Europeanizing the
        native.

XXVII. A NATIVE CLERGY AT LAST   177
        Normal practice of the Church. Neglect of native
        vocations by Portuguese and Spaniards. Efforts of Paris
        Society of Missions. Father Casoria. Stephanie Bigard.
        Father Bataillon in the South Seas. Two Encyclicals on
        the subject. Consecration of six Chinese bishops. Work
        of White Fathers. Native nuns. Catechists.

XXVIII. MEDICAL MISSIONARY SISTERS   181
        Physical healing part of the apostolate. Early examples.
        First Christian Hospitals. Participation by women.
        First Hospitals in the New World. Modern medical
        services. Dr. Agnes McLaren. Protestant enterprise.
        Neglect by Catholics. Dr. McLaren in Kashmir.
        Removal of the ban by Church. Dr. Anna Dengel. First
        Medical Missionary Society. Disease in the Missions.
        Medical Services an act of Restitution. Good in them-
        selves.

XXIX.   EPILOGUE   187

        APPENDIX   191

        INDEX   193

TO THE UTTERMOST PARTS

THE first missionary expedition amounted to no more than a leisurely descent from the top-floor of a house in Jerusalem to the street below where a crowd of Jews, out of every nation under heaven, gathered to hear "the wonderful works of God" described in their own tongues. Next came the formal inauguration of the Christian apostolate by St. Peter, on which occasion three thousand conversions were made.

From now on, the situation develops with remarkable rapidity. Substantial progress is made, not only in the capital, but also in the greater centres both of Judea and of Galilee. At the same time, we have a series of events that set the pattern for all subsequent ages: the truth of the new teaching is demonstrated by a miracle of healing; opposition on the part of the civil power rears its ugly head; there is an enrolment of co-operators or catechists; there is a martyrdom followed by a persecution which is instrumental in carrying the Good Tidings into other lands; and there are differences of opinion among the missionaries themselves.

The seven deacons, who were ordained ostensibly to take charge of the social services now devolving upon the growing community (a kind of Converts' Aid Society), turned out to be much more than dispensers of alms. One of their number, Stephen, preached with inspired persuasiveness and provided Christianity with its first witness-unto-death. Then, when the faithful had to fly from Jerusalem, some of them were escorted into Samaria, the Ulster of Palestine, by the deacon Philip whose discourses won over the greater part of that nation. Other fugitives sought refuge in Antioch, the Beautiful, the one-time capital of Syria, a town about three hundred miles north of Jerusalem and situated in the district now known as Aleppo. Here, the two deacons who led the expedition were the first to plant the seeds of the Gospel in pagan soil.

This latter exodus was destined to have a decisive effect upon the fortunes of the apostolate. Here it was in this Queen of the East, which disputed the claim of Alexandria to be the second city of the Empire, that the missions found their operational headquarters. The business of the Church continued to be transacted in Jerusalem; but the footing there—always precarious—became well-nigh untenable when Herod Agrippa put St. James the Greater, St. John's brother, to death. The same fate threatened St. Peter who escaped by a miraculous deliverance. He joined the growing community in Antioch and, according to a strong tradition, became its first bishop. Here, too, it was that the followers of our Saviour were first called Christians, a designation probably intended as a nickname by the facetious Antiochenes. Here it was that the Apostle of the Gentiles served his apprenticeship and received his commission. It was from Seleucia that the Christian apostolate first took to the sea, and Seleucia was the port of Antioch.

Moreover it is to Antioch that the missionary movement owes its charter of Catholicity as a free-for-all movement; for here arose, and was finally settled, the dispute concerning the relation of the new dispensation to the old, whose outcome was a severance which left the Church free to make her way unhindered. The Twelve seem to have had no thought of attempting the conversion of the Pagan world until after the revelation made to St. Peter at Joppe. Our Lord's last instruction was to the effect that they should bear witness to Him "in Jerusalem, Judea and Samaria, and even to the uttermost parts of the earth." But the Apostles appear to have understood the latter part of the proclamation to refer to the Jews of the dispersion. Then came the vision and the realization that the Gospel message knows neither barriers nor frontiers, but addresses itself to all-and-sundry irrespective of their situation and antecedents; in short, that it was not necessary to be a Jew in order to become a Christian.

Effect was immediately given to this revelation by the reception of the first pagan convert, Cornelius the centurion. But all was not plain-sailing even yet. The question arose: How does this Cornelius, and others like him, stand with regard to the requirements of the Mosaic Law? The Jewish converts had so far refused to sever their connexion with that law; some thought that such a thing could not be done in conscience. The result was that the first Christians, the Apostles included, not only looked like Jews but they acted like Jews. They observed the distinction between clean and unclean food, they refused to eat with and to enter the houses of non-Jews; and, at Jerusalem, they continued to frequent the Temple. Down to date Christianity had the outward appearance of a Jewish sect. Now, along comes this pagan convert and others are sure to follow. What, then, is to be done with them? Since Christianity was a shoot grafted on the Mosaic stem, converts could reach Christ only through Moses. Obviously, then, it was not enough to baptize people like Cornelius; they must be made to comply with the requirements of the Mosaic Law.

Thus arose that first contention, the forerunner of several such, which threatened to end in a deadlock. As it was, it did produce a sect (Jewish Christians), part schismatical, part heretical, that survived into the fifth century.

Fortunately, the controversy came to a head in Antioch, in an atmosphere quite other than that which Jerusalem might have provided. At Antioch, the diehard Judaizers had to reckon with a formidable opposition made up of non-Palestinian Jews (Greeks and Syrians) with whom the Mosaic code never had quite the force of a national law as in the Holy Land. They resented the suggestion that the law of the Gospel was incomplete and needed the reinforcement of the law of Moses. At this juncture, Paul and Barnabas were despatched from Antioch to lay the matter before the Apostles in Jerusalem. The decision was a vindication of the independence and self-sufficiency of the new dispensation. It is no great exaggeration to say, then, that it was in this essentially cosmopolitan city that the cosmopolitan character of Christianity was fully and finally asserted.

Antioch, the first missionary centre in the complete sense, is not a bad observation-post from which to view the progress of the next development—a two-way movement destined to carry the Cross, in the one direction, as far as the Pillars of Hercules and, in the other, through Mesopotamia, Persia, Arabia and beyond; a total distance of about five thousand miles. A ruler and an atlas show Antioch to be equidistant from these extreme points, lying as it does on the dividing line between two worlds; the Mediterranean world of the Roman Empire, and the somewhat shadowy, largely unexplored world identified with the eastern campaigns of Alexander the Great. The double-edged thrust now preparing was to essay the spiritual conquests of both these worlds. Each offensive had the same object in view, and was backed up by the same energy and determination. Yet for a variety of reasons, mainly political and geographical, the eastward drive failed to achieve the rapid and spectacular success which characterized the drive to the west. There is this difference besides, that, whereas the latter is well documented, the former has little history other than a traditionary one and, therefore, its progress is largely a matter of guess work.

As soon as the real nature of their mission had been made known to them, the Apostles resolved to part and go their several ways. Although the merest hint of this break-up is given by St. Luke, a festival in its honour was annually celebrated in parts of Christendom from the eleventh century down almost to modern times. The date usually assigned to this separation is the year 42, which means that it coincided with the start of the missionary journeys of St. Paul. From now on, while the Twelve—as far as the New Testament record goes—practically vanish into thin air, the activities of St. Paul almost monopolize the remaining fifteen chapters of the Acts; naturally enough, surely, since the author was the travelling-companion of the Apostle of the Gentiles, at any rate during most of the time.

It is enough to read this breath-taking narrative to realize how widespread was the penetration made into the Greco-Roman world during the lifetime of that energetic convert. In spite of the impression we have of a man wandering about more or less at random, in reality St. Paul exhibited a strong partiality for one particular piece of territory. In between his two expulsions—from Cyprus, his first objective, and then from Ephesus nine years later—Lesser Asia (represented by modern Turkey) occupied the bulk of his time and attention. All those ancient places with which the Acts have made us familiar—Mysia, Lydia, Pamphylia, Pisidia, Phrygia, Bithynia, Galatia, Iconium, Troas, Cilicia, Cappadocia, Pontus, and so on, were located within the borders of that peninsula sometimes known as Anatolia. When the silversmiths drove the Apostle of the Gentiles from Ephesus, he quitted

Asia Minor for ever, revisited Macedonia and Greece, and settled down to write some of his Epistles. Jerusalem was his next objective. Here he was subjected to a petty persecution which ended in his appeal to Caesar, his safe-conduct to Rome, and the shipwreck on the way that brought him to Malta. He wrote other Epistles during his stay in the Eternal City which he interrupted to visit Crete, and interrupted again, if we are to believe a tradition, to visit Spain. In all these widely-scattered places substantial pioneering work was done, as is proved by the rapid growth of the communities therein established.

But, in spite of the silence surrounding the movements of the other missionaries, it is antecedently most unlikely that St. Paul had the territories of the Roman Empire all to himself. St. Peter's connexion with Rome is no longer questioned, so that Pope Leo's panegyric is valid, on that point at any rate. "O most blessed Apostle! this was the city which thou wert not afraid to enter; alone thou didst penetrate into that forest of wild beasts roaring furiously. Thou didst boldly set up the trophy of the Cross upon those walls within which God's providence appointed the throne of thy honour and the scene of thy martyrdom." The rest of the panegyric embodies traditions which may well be reliable in the main. "Already thou hadst founded the Church of Antioch and promulgated the law of the Gospel through Pontus, Galatia, Cappadocia, Asia and Bithynia." St. John is reputed to have died at Ephesus, as the overseer of all the communities of Asia Minor, which he had previously evangelized almost from end to end; while Judea and Galilee may be accepted as the scene of the labours of St. James the first Bishop of Jerusalem. This is as far as any reliable information goes concerning the operations of the Twelve within the boundaries of the Greco-Roman world.

When we endeavour to ascertain how things have been going on the other, the eastern, side of the barrier—"the mountainous mass of Judaism stretching from Antioch through Jerusalem to Alexandria"—we find ourselves groping in the twilight. Such light as there is comes mostly from traditions of questionable value. What seems, at first glance, to lend support to some of these traditions is the circumstance

2

that, as soon as the regions in question emerge into historical view, we find the Christian faith fairly well established in them; and, along with this faith, its identification with one or other of the Apostles.   But it has to be remembered that claims of this sort are, by their very multiplicity, under grave suspicion. The lack of precise information paved the way for these fictions which grew up everywhere, country vieing with country in an attempt to connect the beginnings of its Christian history with the name of some Apostle or disciple.

There is no doubt that, at an early date, there was a penetration into the country lying north-west of India, and this is associated with the name of St. Bartholomew. Other traditions represent him as having evangelized Mesopotamia, Persia, certain provinces of Asia Minor, the shores of the Black Sea and Armenia, in which last he is said to have been martyred. Ancient writers are at variance as to the countries visited by St. Matthew, but almost all mention the district south of the Caspian Sea known, at that time, as Ethiopia. This tradition is accepted by the Roman Martyrology; other traditions mention Persia and the Parthian Empire which at that time extended as far as the Indian Ocean. St. Simon, the Zealous, is vaguely represented as preaching in many widely scattered lands including Persia. The Armenian Church is certainly of great antiquity (the claim has been advanced that the Armenians were the first people who, as a nation, embraced the faith) and its chief bishop has always described himself as occupying the throne of St. Jude or Thaddeus.

Finally, we have the Thomas-Christians who inhabit the coast of Malabar. We hear tell of them in the sixth century and again (from Marco Polo) in the thirteenth, while Vasco da Gama, in the sixteenth, found them to the number 200,000. According to their own way of it, their forefathers received the faith from the Apostle Thomas who reached them after travelling through Parthia and Arabia. Apart from this belief, there is a vague tradition that St. Thomas visited India, just as there is a vague tradition identifying St. Bartholomew with that country. But in those days the name of India was applied to a number of localities bordering on or even remote from what we know as India; for example, to the south-eastern portion of Arabia, or Arabia Felix, and to Axoum on the Abyssinian coast. It is certain that Christianity found its way into the real India at an early date: Mani, the Persian founder of Manichaeism, preached there in the third century, while the Nestorians evangelized it from Persia later. It may be that these Persian missionaries regarded themselves as the children of St. Thomas, and caused their Indian converts to regard themselves in the same light.

II

CONTRIBUTORY FACTORS

HERE, then, within the space of some twenty or thirty years, we have a geographical expansion unique in the history of the Christian missions. It is not possible to say, with any certainty, what this expansion was worth numerically considered; but we have the well-known testimony of the pagan annalist, Tacitus, to the effect that when Rome, in the person of Nero, made its first move against the new religion, its adherents amounted to a "huge multitude" in the Eternal City alone.

It would be inadvisable to pass on without paying some attention to the factors contributing to this remarkable success. There is agreement among scholars that the principal instrument put into the hands of the first missionaries was the Roman Empire. Although the infant Church was not at all disposed to confine her activities to the imperial framework, it could hardly avoid doing so if there was to be an apostolate at all. Politically, she was under Caesar whose dominions were her fatherland. The organization of the Empire explains, in great measure, the organization of the Church, whose shape and character were cast in the ready-made mould provided by the Greco-Roman culture and civilization. The name given to each Christian congregation was a Greek name (ecclesia), and for long her official language was Greek. Although Christianity had issued out of Judaism and was at first pivoted on Jerusalem and, to a lesser extent, on Caesarea and Antioch, it soon became clear that the choice of these cities was only provisional. In spite of the fact that it was situated beyond the extremity of the Greek world, Rome was the centre towards which, at that date, everything converged. Hence, from the time when the new faith aspired to become a universal religion, it looked very much as though all the Christian roads were destined to lead to Rome. St. Peter's arrival and martyrdom there settled the matter for good and all.

Providentially, the beginning of the apostolate coincided with the consolidation of an Empire which comprehended the fairest portions of the earth, and the most civilized nations of mankind. Gibbon estimates the total number of subjects then acknowledging the imperial laws at 120 millions, "a degree of population forming one of the most numerous societies ever united under a common system of government." "The finger of God", says Newman, "is seen here; politically and geographically, a way had been prepared for the propagation of the Gospel."

There was, first of all, the almost vital matter of communications. There is no comparison, on this score, between the task confronting St. Paul and the task confronting, say, the friars who evangelized the newly-discovered continent of America. He had the solid and guarded highways of the Roman roadmakers, to say nothing of the ready facilities available for those travelling by sea; while the latter had to move, slowly and cautiously, over the face of hostile and almost impassable territories. There do not appear to have been any of the customary casualties among the first missionaries; at least, we do not hear of any having succumbed to the hardships and treacheries of the road. From city to city— that was the itinerary—so much so that Christianity comes before us in the early centuries as a religion of cities. The names of about forty of them are given in the New Testament as having been evangelized, most of them by St. Paul. And these cities were linked up by public thoroughfares which terminated only at the frontiers. This immense chain of communications, stretching from the wall of Antoninus in Scotland, through Rome to Jerusalem, was drawn out to a distance of four thousand and eighty Roman miles. Thanks to the post-houses erected all along these routes, it was possible to travel a hundred miles in one day.

More important still, these roads or sea-routes traversed a world that was at peace. From the Atlantic to the Caspian, from Africa to the shores of Britain, there were no rumours of war; the brigands were under control and the pirates had been swept from the high seas. Never before was intercourse between nation and nation easier and more agreeable. "It is due to the Romans", St. Irenaeus admitted, "that we can travel with impunity, while ships bear us wherever we are pleased to go." We Europeans, for whom even a short holiday abroad involves formidable restrictions and conditions, can hardly realize how accessible to travellers the Greco-Roman world was at that time.

The justly celebrated *Pax Romana* was favourable to the calm consideration of religious topics. There was leisure, and there was a certain absence of temporal strain and anxiety. The learned have not failed to note, besides, the contact that had existed for a long time between Greek thought and Jewish; the Hebrew sacred writings were translated into the Greek tongue about three hundred years previously, so that the educated had some acquaintance with their teaching and prophetic forecasts. St. Paul was, on this account, favourably placed as a missionary, since he was fully conversant with Jewish lore, and with the philosophy and religious mysteries of the Hellenic world. This fact alone goes a fair way to explaining the greater permeability of the Greco-Roman world to the diffusion of the Gospel.

In spite of so many appearances to the contrary, there was, in the Empire, a disposition to tolerate the free discussion of new religious opinions and beliefs. Even in the worst days of the persecution, Christians were still able to defend their convictions before their judges and even by means of books. We are too apt to assume that the imperialism of that age was absolutist in the modern sense. With us, an absolutist régime means a population held down by a standing army, a ubiquitous and secret police, a state monopoly of education, a press censorship and, above all, a bureaucracy backed up by thousands of paid officials whose job it is to manage everything and everyone, and to stamp out each sign and symptom of individual initiative and energy. But the Romans knew nothing of this curious political development. Had their conception of statecraft resembled the samples of it familiar to us, the Christian Church must, humanly speaking, have found it difficult to avoid being stifled almost at birth. The Gospel makes it plain that a man like Pontius Pilate had a far superior sense of fair-play than the Jewish officials with whom he was in collision.

The dispersed Jewish communities were another important asset, since, through them, contacts and even conversions were guaranteed in advance. Although the majority were congregated in the West, we know that on the Day of Pentecost, the Holy City harboured pilgrims of every nation under heaven including Parthia, Media, Elam, Mesopotamia and Arabia. We know from other accounts that, beyond the frontiers, there were whole districts inhabited by Jews; there had been repeated deportations into the remote regions of Asia, to say nothing of the dispersion of the Ten Tribes at an early date. At Antioch they were in a majority, and at Alexandria they constituted two-fifths of the population. It was not easy to find a locality in the Empire where there were no Jews, and their influence was far in excess of their numbers. They possessed synagogues and, in some places—in Egypt notably—they possessed great wealth. They made many proselytes especially among well-to-do women; and this, because their doctrine of the divine unity appealed to many of those amongst their pagan neighbours who were sick and tired of the classic mythology, with its welter of gods and goddesses.

And it was on these communities that the first missionaries relied for hospitality and a send-off, especially St. Paul, who comes before us first in the synagogue at Cyprus to which he had journeyed in the company of Barnabas, a Cyprian Jew, and last as interviewing his fellow Jews in a hired lodging at Rome. He seems to have had no difficulty in finding accommodation wherever he went—a testimony to the strength of the racial bond binding this people together under all circumstances. One likes to think of him as setting out equipped with letters of introduction and a list of names and addresses. And although these Jewish emigrants were attached to the traditions and rites of their religion, they were more open to persuasion than their brethren in the home-land. It was probably easier to convert an Alexandrian Jew than a Palestinian one.

St. Augustine described the advent of the Gospel teaching as *a timely* intervention, a work of rescue undertaken in the nick of time. Much has been made of the moral and spiritual anarchy of the ancient pagan world. All the same, we are not to picture that world as utterly sunk in depravity of mind and conscience. Modern missionaries know how formidable an obstacle such radical decadence opposes to the success of their labours; they have to civilize before they can convert, have to begin by establishing elementary principles of decency. But the ancient culture—at any rate before the decline set in —was characterized by a certain nobility and high-mindedness; a monumental quality. These pagans worshipped and prayed, and their daily life was hallowed by a liturgy; and this routine imparted to that culture of theirs a sacredness before which we feel ourselves compelled to linger in reverence. They had a firmer grasp and a clearer insight into fundamentals than many of our contemporaries in the so-called Christendom of today. They were dignified by a notable simplicity of soul, the absence of which, in our time, makes the inculcation of religious truths supremely difficult; the Greeks especially, whose very language was conspicuous for its honest straightforwardness.

There was among them, too, a longing for enlightenment and moral liberation. One can see from their best writings how sincere and acute this longing was, how energetic were the efforts made by superior minds to pierce the darkness that enveloped the basic problems of life and death. Some of their poets gave such clear and touching expression to this mood that they have been called the "Prophets of the human race in its natural condition". These thinkers had reached a stage beyond which their speculations refused to go. They were tantalized by the gaps and discrepancies perceptible in their own theories and systems. A man like Socrates was forced to the conclusion that the human intellect was, as far as theological matters went, at the end of its tether. They felt, as we feel, that human life is, to a disquieting extent, subjected to the mysterious and malignant law of necessity. Not being in a position to invoke a higher law, they fell back upon that fatalism which is only a thinly disguised despair. The Stoics took refuge in an artificial and cultivated resignation or indifference. They strove to put sequence and order and stability into the scheme of things, only to find necessity still enthroned as the sovereign ruler. High moral ideas they were able to envisage and to cherish, but they could not get them to work; the great weakness of their morality was its practical weakness. Plato was not able to find fifty families with which to realize his Ideal Republic. On those proud and cultivated lips a cry for deliverance was beginning to take shape: "Who shall free us from the body of this death?" The new faith came in response to that cry, in response to the need, widely felt at this time, for some sort of *intervention*, even divine intervention.

As for the world of Judaism, through which Christian truth had to pass on its way to the Gentiles, that too was ripe for a spiritual rehabilitation. To the Chosen People, God had never ceased to manifest Himself, renewing again and again the promise of a Redeemer and Deliverer. Just as there were, among us, far-seeing individuals who prepared our minds for the recent war and for the social upheaval that followed it, so they had had the benefit of a whole series of inspired forecasts all tending in one direction. When at length the nation was compelled to pay tribute to Caesar and the sceptre passed from the land of Juda, the Rabbis made proclamation that the time was at hand; and Malachy, the last of a long line of prophets, uttered a final warning: "Presently the Lord whom you seek shall come to His temple". This was the time-signal in Israel.

No one would suggest that what is here set out is a good and sufficient explanation of the phenomenon of the Church's rapid development during those first years. That would be to fall into the error of the author of *The Decline and Fall of the Roman Empire*. In a memorable part of this work, he reviews what he calls the secondary causes of the expansion of the Christian faith, and these causes he reduces to five. Considered in themselves as factors favouring the growth of the new religion, it is impossible to find fault with them, and they might well make their way into the most orthodox manual of Church History. What is objectionable in Gibbon is, first, the latent sarcasm of his tone, and, next, the artful manner in which he so manipulates his argument as to create around his subject an atmosphere of doubt and suspicion. Having analysed the whole objectionable passage, Newman sums up as follows: "We have to determine whether those five characteristics of primitive Christianity (the zeal of the first converts, their pure and austere morals, their union and discipline, and so on) were sufficient causes of bodies of men becoming Christians. I think they neither did *effect* such conversions, nor were adapted to do so."

In a striking passage, Harnack vindicates the truth of the matter for all time. He shows how Christianity established itself, not only thanks to the employment of every force and every form, but, primarily, owing to what it was in *itself*, and, hence, owing to the impression it produced upon the ancient world. "Everything," he says, "which can be conceived of as religion, it is; everything which can be called religion, it possesses; so much so, that all the known religions appeared poor and necessitous in relation to it." And he concludes: "It is impossible to embrace this unique religion with one glance; nevertheless a single name sums it up—that of Jesus Christ."

III

THE FIRST MISSIONARIES AND THEIR METHODS

WHILE it is usually unsafe to argue from the silences of history, on the other hand the very volubility of history may lead to top-heavy conclusions. These two cautions are necessary when we attempt to apportion the credit for the extension of Christ's Kingdom during the first few decades; and, indeed, during every subsequent decade.

It is impossible to exaggerate the importance of St. Paul who was, and will always be regarded as, *the* missionary *par excellence*, the one who thought in terms of those Roman provinces through which he passed like a meteor. As though to compensate posterity for the obscurity that surrounds the activities of his colleagues, providence willed to provide St. Paul with a publicity-agent who allowed little to escape his vigilant eye. St. Paul himself did the rest; his letters and discourses, for all their objectivity, partake of the nature of autobiography. Whereas the others present themselves to our imagination as somewhat shadowy figures, we cannot think of him at all save as one overwhelmingly substantial, real and personal; as of an individual whom we have known all our lives. It is still possible to write an exhaustive character-study of the Apostle of the Gentiles, but it would not be easy to render a similar service to St. Matthew, say, or even to St. Peter. Confining ourselves to the apostolate, it must be allowed that St. Paul was in advance of the others in his recognition of its implications as an offer of salvation to all without distinction. As one scholar says: "By making a clean sweep of the ancient privileges of Israel, and by enabling the newly-born Church to detach itself from the synagogue, he led Christianity to define itself more sharply, and to enter resolutely on the path marked out for it by its Founder."

For all that, lavish are the praises bestowed, and justly bestowed, upon the Twelve by the writers and preachers of the primitive Church. They are not just Messengers of the Gospel, but Christ's own deputed and accredited Messengers. He is from God and they are from Him—"both these things follow in good order". They are the Lights of the world, because they were the means whereby the Lord was pleased to deliver the nations from darkness; they are the Salt of the earth, because through them they that dwell upon the earth tasted the savour of life eternal. If Christ be the Inner Door they are the Gates. He is the corner-stone of the edifice, they the foundations; the Twelve Foundations which the Scripture ascribes to the City. Their very number has a deep mystical significance worked out in the Divine Mind. "From the four winds of the earth the nations are to be gathered together, and gathered in the name of the Three in one; now Four being multiplied by Three are Twelve." Many and very many were called, or felt called, to the duty of spreading the Good News in however humble a capacity or remote a corner. But they were *chosen* and chosen by our Lord in person (His first choice) by means of a series of formal declarations designed to give point and prominence to the delegation.

But, then, as though to put us on our guard against the omissions of history, the same Master almost immediately made choice of a second delegation the names of whose members are unknown. To the identity and function of the Seventy-Two we have no clue of any kind. It is evident that they were a band of pioneers sent in advance into the surrounding towns and villages to make straight the way of the Lord; but this is all that is reported of them. One ancient document gives to the selection a symbolical signification. If we take it that the choice of *twelve* Apostles indicated the mission of Christianity to the Jewish nation—the twelve tribes of Israel—then the choice of these coadjutors may have an oblique reference to the seventy-two peoples who, according to contemporary Jewish and Christian belief, made up the population of the world at that time.

Every account of missionary work, no matter which period it covers, ought to devote a chapter to the heroic and inglorious band of the anonymous. Apropos of the service Mary Magdalen rendered to His Sacred Body, our divine Lord promised that, wheresoever His Gospel would be preached, the story of that service would be told to preserve her memory. Fortunate Mary Magdalen! But up and down that first-century world of Jew and Gentile, there must have been hundreds of devotees doing what they could—in the market place, at housedoors, in camps and prisons and workshops—to build up His Mystical Body, whereas they themselves were destined to remain unpublicized.

Even a superficial acquaintance with the subject matter of this book—which is all that the writer has to his credit—reveals the presence of these off-stage performers toiling in the background. One big reason why the seeds of the Word took root so quickly in certain places was that the soil had been prepared beforehand. St. Paul might tell the Corinthians that he had planted, Apollo watered and God given the increase; but this was by no means the whole of the transaction in every case. The first diffusion of Christianity was not the work of missionaries at all, but of those Jewish travellers and pilgrims from every nation under heaven who had been in Jerusalem for the festival, and carried away to their adopted countries the report of the Pentecostal miracle and preaching. When St. Paul arrived in Puteoli on his way to Rome, he found those there whom the *Acts* describes as "brethren". If, as seems likely, these brethren were Christian believers, there is no knowing how or by whom they were initiated.

What our Blessed Lady did in this way can only be matter of conjecture; but it is a fairly sound conjecture, surely. From the time of her Son's Ascension until her death, she has always been thought of as more or less nursing the infant Church. It is true that the Gospel speaks of her taciturnity, of how she kept her thoughts to herself; but no woman will consent to do that indefinitely, where the matters in question are vitally connected with her own flesh and blood. Precise information is forthcoming concerning the part played by the man who was born blind, and by her who was converted at the Well of Samaria. She, indeed, may be regarded as the first in that long and noble succession of women-folk who have served the missions in every age, and never more heroically than in our own. Among her countrymen, her ready tongue had so effectively prepared the way of the Lord that when, at their own request, He went amongst them, He met with a better response than in Israel. "Thus, what is often interpreted as a weakness and a reproach against women—that they cannot keep things to themselves—is a noble testimony to the suitability of women for work in the propagation of the Kingdom of God."

Perhaps this is as good a place as any for reminding ourselves that, in the early Service Books of the Christian Church, the work of converting the heathen was regarded as being especially the work of queens. At the coronation of a queen, after putting the ring on her finger, the bishop prayed that she might be enabled "to call the barbarous nations to the knowledge of the truth". And, sure enough, in the history of the apostolate, we find an astonishing number of these same royal personages exercising this prerogative of theirs in a most decisive way. What Bertha, Ethelbert's consort, did for England, and Clovis' wife, Clotilde, did for the Franks is known to all. And there were others besides these: Theodolinda, the Bavarian Princess who converted her husband Agilulf, the Lombard, and so Christianized the whole of his subjects; Olga, who introduced the Gospel into Russia; Dubrawka, who induced the Duke of Bohemia, her husband, to receive baptism—an event leading to the conversion of his nation. Bogoris of Bulgaria and Bulgaria itself owed the faith, in the first instance, to the good office of his sister; while Lithuania was led into the Church through the conversion of King Jagello, whom Hedwig of Poland refused to marry until he had been baptized.

We are reminded by a competent authority that the oriental cults that spread through the Empire at this time did so thanks to the chance encounters and casual gossip of travellers, soldiers, merchants and slaves; and, he remarks, we need not be astonished to find providence using similar means to make Christianity known to the Jewish and pagan world. It was only to be expected that the new creed should gain a ready footing in the Roman armies, as in fact it did. Owing to the troubled state of Palestine, there were more soldiers quartered there, in proportion, than in any other locality with the exception of Britain. Some of these were witnesses of the crucifixion of One whose character and teaching were already familiar to them. A miracle of healing converted the Centurion. Again, St. Paul spent a considerable time in the company of these legionaries. During his long imprisonment, he was in their charge; and, we may be sure, made the most of such an opportunity. We can imagine what the effect must have been of the discussions and exchanges carried on by these men among their comrades, and among the acquaintances they made as they moved from province to province. We know that Cappadocia owed much to the Thundering Legion quartered there during the reign of Marcus Aurelius, many of whose soldiers were Christians. We know again that the Christian prisoners carried from Syria to Mesopotamia by Sapor, after his victory in 260, made their influence felt in the place of their internment. The early Martyrologies contain the names of quite a number of soldiers whose conversion and martyrdom almost coincided, and one may conclude that some of these had had their attention drawn to the new faith by their companions-in-arms.

All sorts of others there were, too; martyrs testifying before their judges and accusers, wives predisposing their husbands to a favourable reception of the Good Tidings, and slaves gaining over their masters and mistresses. In the fourth century we hear of the Queen of the Marcomanni writing to ask St. Ambrose to send missionaries to her country (Bohemia), a request obviously inspired by some influence—a humble influence perhaps—in or about her court. There are very good grounds for believing that the kingdom of Iberia or Georgia was converted about this time, through the influence of a female slave whose prayers were thought to have cured the queen of an illness. In the reign of Constantine, the Gospel was brought to the Abyssinians by two slaves, one of whom became the first bishop of that territory. Authentic history records the apostolic activities even of a small boy of twelve, namely, St. Ansanus the Martyr, who, having been disowned by his well-to-do pagan parents, converted so many in the neighbourhood of Siena that he became known as The Baptizer.

Although these instances belong to a later date, they help us to appreciate what must have been going on everywhere during the period now under review. Justice can be done to this side of the apostolate without falling back on the legends at all. These multiplied to such a degree that, in the end, there was hardly a locality that failed to connect the beginning of its faith with some picturesque personage. Thus the charioteer of

Queen Candace, whom Philip baptized, was credited with the first evangelization of African Ethiopia; while the first Bishop of Limoges was reputed to be no other than the boy with the loaves and fishes mentioned in the Gospel. There is, besides, the tradition associating the conversion of southern Gaul with Martha and Mary and their brother Lazarus; and so on.

The *Acts* give us a number of specimen discourses addressed to Jewish audiences with a view to their conversion. The gist of the argument employed is that the promises and prophecies of the Old Law find their evident fulfilment in Christ. This is the substance of the Pentecostal sermon of St. Peter, upon whom devolved the duty of making the first excursion into the field of Christian apologetics. At Joppe, the same Peter concludes his account of our Lord's ministry with the statement: "In Him all the prophets give testimony". This was the line taken by St. Paul in the synagogue at Antioch in Pisidia. Usually the moral drawn is: "Repent and be baptized", a twofold appeal readily appreciated by the Jews to whom the need of regeneration by a change of life was strongly felt at that time, and to whom the symbolism of baptism was familiar. In the second century, this procedure was elaborated by Justin Martyr, who insists that the followers of Christ are the true children of Israel, and that Christianity enables Judaism to realize itself as a universal religion, which the true religion ought to be.

From a rich variety of sources, information is forthcoming regarding the method of dealing with the pagan world. To begin with, there is St. Paul's speech to the Athenians in which he uses the tablet-inscription TO THE UNKNOWN GOD as the basis of his argumentation. For all its achievements, Greek philosophy was still groping and searching; therefore, perhaps, willing and even eager to be taught. What else, after all, was that philosophy but plain evidence of the need the human had of the divine; it was man trying to raise himself to the level from which he had fallen. But here was the God incarnate placing Himself at his disposal; His resurrection and ascension were guarantees of their own, could they but be brought to unite themselves with Him. Something, too, may be learned from the testimonies delivered by the martyrs in presence of their judges. The classic example is that of St. Apollonius, a Roman senator well versed in philosophy, who suffered about the year 190. After some preliminary argumentation, the judge asked the prisoner to explain his point of view, which he did in a speech of moving simplicity and power. In describing our Lord, he uses a phraseology familiar to the educated world of the time: "He is the *Word* of God who brought into existence men's souls and bodies. Filled with divine wisdom, He taught us the two things that thinkers, so far, had failed to teach: what God is really like, and what the end and object of virtue really is. And whereas the pagan moralists could only *inculcate* the practice of virtue, He puts us in the way of doing it. Just as Socrates was unjustly condemned, so was the Saviour; but Christians worship Him, because they are under no delusions as to what and who He was."

Early on, however, it was found necessary to compile and circulate formal publications which the educated public could ponder at their leisure. They were known as *Apologies*. The men who wrote them were recent converts, well versed in the classic culture and, therefore, familiar with both sides. They usually begin by challenging paganism on its own ground, the ground of natural philosophy. The ethical purity of Christianity is stressed, evidently with an eye to the Stoics whose system was widely current at the time. Origen, to give one instance, exposes the palpable weakness of the pagan system of religion, and shows how futile was the high-minded moralizing of its philosophers; only two, he says, were rescued from their depravities by the teachings of Plato. Then he bids his opponent ponder the contrast which Christ's teaching exhibits in this respect, how its intrinsic worth and power have reformed the lives of countless thousands belonging to every class and condition.

Since the acceptance of Christianity involved belief in a definite body of doctrine, some sort of preliminary religious instruction was considered necessary from the beginning. In the case of the first converts, this was provided by those powerful discourses which, as we saw, brought them into the fold in thousands; their good dispositions were so manifest that they were baptized at once. Philip explained the passage of Isaias to Queen Candace's man-of-business, and preached

3

Jesus unto him; whereupon the latter asked, "What is to prevent me from being baptized?" And Philip told him that there was nothing, provided he believed with all his heart that Jesus was the Son of God. And when he answered that he did so believe, they both went down into the water where Philip baptized him. It is very unlikely, though, that these new Christians would be left to fend for themselves. Already in the Epistle to the Galatians we hear of official instructors or catechists.

But when the communities began to be organized and, more especially, when the persecution broke out, a period of probationary instruction was found to be a plain matter of prudence. In his apology, Justin the Martyr tells how "those who are persuaded and believe are *taught* to ask for the remission of their sins, after which they are led to a place where there is water and so baptized". By the end of Justin's century, the second, the catechumenate was in force. If a pagan wished to become a Christian, he was given some elementary instruction, his conduct was watched meanwhile, and he was allowed to be present at a part of the Eucharistic service. If his instructors were satisfied that he was in earnest, he was then put among the catechumens and allowed to call himself a Christian, as distinct from one of the "faithful". The catechumenate might last a long time, as much as eight months for Jews and two years for pagans. In some cases the catechumens put off their baptism for years; SS. Ambrose, Basil, Gregory Nazianzen and John Chrysostom were not baptized until after their thirtieth year, although meanwhile they were regarded as Christians.

As to the quality of the first converts, the Christian spokesmen admit that they were drawn, for the most part, from the humbler ranks of society. This circumstance they turn into an argument, because it was notorious that pagan philosophy had no message for the poor and illiterate. Lactantius told the well-to-do that they were handicapped by the cares and riches of this world, as the Parable had foretold. At the same time, St. Augustine, with a dry humour, was able to boast that the Gospel fishermen had gone out and caught fish of every kind, including that most rare and wonderful species of fish, the philosophers themselves. Among these were Quadratus,

Aristides, Justin, Melito, Athenagoras, Pantaenus, Clement of Alexandria, Tertullian, Origen, Heraclas, Dionysius, Minucius Felix, and so on. There were many notable people besides; for example, the chamberlain of the Ethiopian queen, the foster-brother of Herod, the governor of Cyprus, the senators Pudens and Apollonius, the centurion Cornelius, Crispus the ruler of the synagogue at Corinth, the consul Flavius Clemens, the nephew of the emperor Vespasian, Glabrio, Flavian's colleague, St. Felicity and her seven sons, and those to whom St. Paul refers as the Household of Caesar.

IV

THE SUB-APOSTOLIC AGE

I F the documents have little to tell of the first Christian missionaries, this comparative silence extends to the record of the succeeding or sub-apostolic age. We find the Gospel gradually extending its conquests through the near East and making astonishing headway in the West, but we are left very much in the dark concerning both the agents and the processes employed in carrying the work through. For the most part, we are presented with a *fait accompli* whose antecedents are shrouded in obscurity. Writing of the second century, Eusebius the Church-historian remarks that "there were many disciples of the Apostles then living who, upon the foundations laid by them, built splendid edifices of the faith, everywhere preaching the Word of God and scattering broadcast over the earth the fruitful seed of the Kingdom of heaven". To supplement this very general statement there are only traditions; those, for example, associating the foundation of the see of Paris with Denis the Areopagite, that of Marseilles and Narbonne with Crescentius, the disciple of St. Paul, and that of Arles with Trophimus, the disciple of St. Peter. Another tradition credits the latter with sending Spain its first seven bishops.

The evangelization of Africa has no history, neither has that of Spain or Britain; and the same may be said of other localities. By the close of the third century there were in Egypt numerous Christian villages and bishops, yet we have no knowledge of how this notable result was brought about. In the same way, Spanish Christianity does not come into clear view until the Council of Elvira, at which a large number of bishops assembled. By that time the entire country had been evangelized; but when or by whom is a mystery. Indeed, the first example of a missionary enterprise that is properly documented would appear to be that of St. Augustine to England.

Père Battifol says of this period that the propagation of the faith was not the work of missionaries, and that St. Paul had no successors in the centuries immediately following his exertions. Such results as were achieved were due, as far as we know, to the labours of individual bishops who naturally regarded the winning over of the heathen as a vital part of their duty. In the second century, we hear tell of St. Irenaeus, Bishop of Lyons, labouring among the Celts in the surrounding country, and labouring so constantly that his Greek was suffering. St. Martin of Tours was another notable apostle of the countryside. He quitted his solitude at Ligugé (the Gallic Thebaid) and traversed the forest-land of central and western Gaul, preaching to the rough and ready peasants of that region and winning them over to the faith. Even today it is possible to trace the routes he followed, thanks to the legends of which he is the hero. Missionaries had recourse to him for instruction, amongst them maybe St. Ninian who dedicated his church at Whithorn to St. Martin.

There were exceptions of course, and one notable free-lance apostle is Pantaenus who was head of the great School at Alexandria about the year 180. He set out on a long missionary expedition which carried him as far as "India" (probably southern Arabia) where he found Christians in possession of a Gospel of St. Matthew, written in Hebrew, which they maintained had been given to their forefathers by St. Bartholomew. The monks of the Thebaid, too, rendered a valuable service to the cause, for large numbers of them preached the faith in Phoenicia on the one side, and beyond the Euphrates on the other.

It is not until the fourth century, however, that we find anything like concerted and organized efforts. Round about the year 370, the Bishop of Vercelli established a training college alongside his cathedral, from which catechists went out into the surrounding districts. It was in this way that the valley of the Po was evangelized and its first sees founded. A little later, St. John Chrysostom did the same thing in Constantinople, providing educational facilities for native Goths, who thus qualified themselves to preach the Gospel to their heathen countrymen. In some of his Letters we find information concerning the movements of these missionaries, as well as appeals for money for their support. It is not inappropriate to mention that the collecting-boxes to be found in many of our Christian houses, a good proportion of which are sponsored by missionary organizations, appear to have originated with this saint or, at any rate, in his time. In one of his sermons he exhorts the faithful to make use of this device in order to sanctify the domestic circle and give wings to their prayers. It was at this very time, too, that Honoratus erected his abbey on the islet of Lérins near Toulon, and this soon developed into a missionary training-ground and the parent of others in southern and western Gaul.

During the first two centuries of our era, the most considerable body of Christians was to be found in the rich provinces extending from Mesopotamia to the western boundary of Greece proper. Construed in terms of modern geography, this immense territory very roughly corresponds to the Turkish or Ottoman Empire as it was almost within living memory. Although there was opposition to contend with in Palestine, in Syria there were already very formidable communities, especially in Antioch which, before the end of the fourth century, contained about one hundred thousand Christians. The Book of Revelations gives prominence to the seven chief Churches of Asia Minor, each of which was a centre from which missionary activity radiated in every direction. Powerful Christian groups had, by now, grown up in Cyprus, Crete, Thrace, Macedonia and in the cities of Athens, Sparta and Corinth; while things were equally prosperous in the Danubian regions of Dalmatia and Illyricum.

But for sheer density of population relative to the size of the territory, North Africa came first. Tertullian contended that Christians were so numerous here that their deportation would mean the closing down of municipal life and activity. Even allowing for his exaggeration, it is likely that believers were in a majority in the cities; that they belonged to all classes the Acts of the martyrdoms show. There were more bishops here than in Gaul or Upper Italy. Missionary enterprise extended as far as Mauretania (Algiers and Oran) and even beyond the Sahara. Abyssinia was almost won over as early as the reign of Constantine, and Nubia was evangelized a century later. Egypt was, of course, the stronghold of the African Church and had a hundred dioceses before the end of the third century.

Until the second century the history of Christianity in

Italy is largely the history of the community in the city of Rome. Then we find two more bishoprics, Milan and Ravenna; and in another hundred years eight more, namely Aquileia, Verona and Brescia in the north, and Ostia, Porto, Albano, Tibur and Naples in the south. After that comes an amazing spurt which results in no fewer than sixty bishops putting in an appearance at a synod held in Rome in 251. At this time it is calculated that there were forty thousand Christians in Rome alone.

Of course, such information as we have has to do with cities; and, in fact, it is conceded that little progress had so far been made in the country parts. In this respect the eastern apostolate greatly differed from that of the west. As late as the sixth century, we find Pope Gregory rebuking Italian land-owners for neglecting to convert their peasants, and advising one Italian bishop to make a start himself by preaching the Gospel to the rustics who, he says, ought to be fined, imprisoned or chastised should they refuse to listen. Then, again, when we hear of episcopal sees being multiplied, we have to remember that their numerical importance is not thereby guaranteed since, in those days, bishops ruled over small communities.

Long before the close of the second century, the Christians of Gaul were numerous enough to attract the special attention of the persecutor. We say the Christians of Gaul, but a better name for them would be the Christians of Lyons. At that time, Lyons was to Gaul what Rome was to Italy; its bishop was styled Bishop of the Church of Gaul. In this persecution of the year 177, that city provided forty-eight martyrs. Although its beginnings are vague and uncertain, the likelihood is that Gaul's first missionaries came from the East. The first two bishops of that see were disciples of St. Polycarp of Smyrna; St. Martin of Tours himself being a native of Pannonia (Hungary). They would disembark at Marseilles, and then push on up the Rhone to Lyons, the metropolis and centre of communications for the whole country.

By the end of the fourth century, Gaul had been at least superficially evangelized as far as the Alpine cantons. Here again, however, not a great deal had been done for the rustic population, since at the close of the fourth century we find one

missionary explaining to his country audience that the sign
of the Cross is the sign of the God who alone is worshiped by
those dwelling in the large cities. No great progress was made
in this direction until the monks came along, and carried their
monastic establishments into the heart of the huge forests
which covered Gaul at that period.

About Spain, such information as is available tells very
much the same story. Prudentius, who was himself a Spaniard,
assures us that his countrymen distinguished themselves as
martyrs in every one of the persecutions. The findings of the
Council of Elvira were signed by nineteen bishops. This was in
the year 300.

Turning to the East, whatever may have been the origins
of the Christian communities of Persia, apostolic or otherwise,
there is no doubt that, by the beginning of the third century,
they had grown to a considerable size. The Persian kings at
this period favoured or, at least, tolerated the new religion,
and during the persecutions many refugees flowed into their
territory unmolested. They were free to build churches of
their own and did do so, it is claimed, to the number of about
three hundred and sixty.

We may note here that the settlement which put western
Christendom on its feet, was a great set-back to the Christians
of Persia. That Church was of Syrian origin, and regarded
Antioch as the centre of its faith and the seat of its authority;
a state of affairs which was, politically, highly satisfactory,
since Persia and Rome were enemies. Constantine's conversion, and the subsequent protectorship of the Church which he
assumed, roused the jealousy and hostility of the Persian
monarchs, and started a bitter persecution which lasted for
one hundred years. Christianity, however, not only held its
own but continued to extend itself in many directions. From
the time of its importation from Egypt, in this same century,
monasticism spread rapidly through Persia proper, Armenia,
Mesopotamia and the regions north of the Tigris. There is
evidence, too, that many of these monks were active in the
work of evangelizing the pagan parts of their adopted country.

The fourth century had hardly opened when Christianity
was proclaimed the state religion of Armenia. The man
responsible for this achievement, the first of its kind in order

of time, was St. Gregory the Illuminator, the son of a Parthian prince, who baptized the king and the royal family, and is said to have consecrated 400 bishops. To the north of Armenia, on the south side of the Caucasus mountains, lay Iberia or Georgia which soon after entered the lists as a converted nation. Missionaries from this wild district carried the Gospel westwards as far as Albania. Meanwhile, a steady development was going on down in southern Arabia where already, in the second century, Bosra was an episcopal centre of importance. A successful apostolate was carried on later by a bishop whom the Emperor Constans sent thither for the purpose.

Gibbon calculates that about one-twentieth part of the subjects of the Empire had enrolled themselves under the banner of the Cross before the conversion of Constantine, and that the faith of Christ had found its way into every city and province of the Empire. From the second century onwards, we find the Christian apologists using this diffusion as an argument, a risky thing to do had they not been sure of their facts. But, indeed, the facts were not questioned, for history records a number of reluctant admissions which are to the effect that Christianity is practically having things its own way.

One of the earliest defenders of the Christian cause defies his adversary to find any known race of people, whether Greek or Barbarian, whether city-dwellers or nomads, among whom prayers are not offered to God in the name of His Son, the crucified Jesus. In the next century, Origen extols the disinterestedness of the preachers of the Gospel who, he says, are spreading the faith in every region, not only through the cities, but even through the towns and villages, in spite of the fact that they are often short of the necessaries of life. His point about the towns and villages is significant, for it shows that already, at this early stage, the Cross was boldly advancing from the security of the cities into the countryside, the last stronghold of paganism. Less than a hundred years later St. Athanasius, exercising no doubt a good deal of oratorical liberty, speaks as though the work had already been done; everywhere the sun is shining, everywhere the idols have been routed or overthrown. "Who," he asks, "before

Christ, ever reached and influenced the Scythian, the Ethiopian, the Persian, the Armenian, the Goth, the islander of the ocean and the Hyrcanians (who dwelt near the Caspian), or discoursed against idolatry with men of such uncouth morals and manners as the Egyptians and Chaldeans?"

V

THE PROS AND CONS OF THIS PERIOD

THIS rapid propagation of a difficult faith was an outstanding achievement, viewed in itself. What renders it
unique in missionary annals is the circumstance that it was
carried on in the face of a very determined opposition; and an
opposition that, as far as material resources went, had the
field to itself. It is not often that the Church is allowed to
make "peaceful penetrations"; she was certainly not allowed
to make them in the first few centuries of her existence. The
Great Persecution lasted, on and off, for two and a half
centuries; during which period there were—it has been
calculated—some 129 years of actual persecution. The
details of its cruelties are familiar to everybody. St. Paul
must have had a good idea of what was coming when,
in his Letter to the Corinthians, he spoke of the heroism of
the missionary's vocation.

"It seems to me as if God had destined us His apostles to
be in the lowest place of all, like men under sentence of death;
such a spectacle do we present to the whole creation, men and
angels alike. We are fools for Christ's sake, you are so wise;
we are so helpless, you so stout of heart; you are held in
honour, while we are despised. Still, as I write, we go hungry
and thirsty and naked; we are mishandled, we have no home
to settle in; we are hard put to it, working with our own
hands. Men revile us, and we answer with a blessing; persecute
us, and we make the best of it; speak ill of us, and we fall to
entreaty. We are still the world's refuse, and everybody thinks
himself well rid of us."

But there was more to it than torturing and killing.
Extremely repressive laws were promulgated and put into
force the object of which was to make the profession or, at
least, the practice of the new faith a practical impossibility.
The Christian apologist boasted that all this bloodshed
succeeded in doing the very opposite of what it planned to do.
As a general statement this can well stand, although there is
evidence that in certain localities, in North Africa certainly,
the rate of progress was appreciably slowed down during the

persecutions, only to be greatly accelerated during the intervals of peace. It is notorious, too, that there were apostasies; the disciplinary enactments of the Church show this, as well as the development of the catechumenate which aimed at diminishing the number of these failures. But we can see from the Acts of the Martyrs that there was usually someone whom God inspired to step into the shoes vacated by those whose courage proved unequal to the test. The spectacle of the martyr's constancy produced many conversions. The Roman Martyrology keeps, on December 10th, the festival of a platoon of soldiers detailed to escort some Christians to the place of execution, at a town called Leontium in Sicily. The constancy of the victims so moved the soldiers that they declared their faith and suffered death immediately.

Fire and sword were not the only things the young Church had to contend with. There were few districts in Christendom —Gaul was one of them—which did not at this time exhibit the regrettable spectacle of discordant creeds and multiplying denominations. In certain places, notably in Africa, the heretical bishops outnumbered the orthodox ones. When St. Gregory Nazianzen began his ministry in Constantinople, the Arians were in possession of all its churches. Many a proud record and fair copybook was spoilt and blotted, that of Antioch, for instance, where the confusion was extreme. For a time Rome itself was the seat of three different schismatical bishops, besides the legitimate one. Newman, in the last book he wrote as an Anglican, enumerates these disorders in a lengthy and striking paragraph; and, in a subsequent chapter, he remarks that these sects contained elements of truth amid their error; and had Christianity been as they, it might have resolved into them. As it was, however, it had a hold of the truth which gave its teaching a gravity, consistency and force to which its rivals, for the most part, were strangers.

As far as geographical extension goes this penetration is probably unique in the history of the Christian missionary movement. St. Patrick is considered to have converted Ireland within his own lifetime, but Ireland is only a tight little island after all. It took eighty years to convert England, and certain portions of the South American continent are not properly converted yet. And, besides, there are a number of considerations which combine to throw the achievement of the Apostles' immediate successors into very high relief.

The Church has nothing so much at heart as the extension of Christ's Kingdom. She is under sealed orders to increase and multiply and fill the earth. From the beginning, prayers for the conversion of unbelievers were recognized as proper to Christian devotion, and are to be found in the liturgies of the East and West. Hence St. Augustine asks: "Was there ever a time when petition was not made in the Church for infidels that they might believe?" The earliest mention of this practice seems to occur in the Letter St. Ignatius wrote to the Christians of Ephesus: "Pray without ceasing for the rest of mankind, for there is in them a hope of repentance, that they may attain to God". It is clear, also, that from the earliest times pagan outsiders had access to the part of Christian worship that consisted of instruction; at the end of the fourth century, among the rules drawn up at the Council held in Carthage is one warning bishops not to hinder the heathen, heretic or Jew from entering the church to hear the word of God.

Yet the Church—always and everywhere—is compelled to operate her apostolate within, or in subordination to, existing conditions. Although the Missal contains a Collect in which God is asked to give her liberty to discharge her mission, rarely has she been granted anything like a full measure of that same liberty. Her permanent problem in the mission field is political interference; sometimes well-meaning, sometimes ill-meaning. The result is much the same in either case; she has suffered almost as much from political patronage as from political hostility.

Happily, in this first epoch, the Gospel message presented itself to the world divested of all "strings", entanglements, material inducements and what we may term negative incentives. We know that in the case of America the sword opened up the way for the Cross; the missionaries, at any rate until the Jesuits arrived in North America, were invariably accompanied by soldiers. We know, too, that, although there is little evidence of actual coercion, the natives were baptized wholesale, and baptized often without having much choice. But in the apostolic and sub-apostolic age it was otherwise. And there was no political pressure such as that associated with Constantine and his successors, and associated again to a disquieting degree with Charlemagne and the Frankish monarchs generally. Even the modern missions, that is to say those dating from the nineteenth century onwards, in which there is to be found as much self-sacrificing heroism as in any period, have been overshadowed by the hard fact of western aggression and acquisitiveness.

But the labours of the first missionaries were absolutely disinterested, not only in fact but also in appearance. They marched under no flag, and were under compliment to no interested parties of any kind. As Doctor Johnson wrote with characteristic bluntness, "These first propagators of Christianity entered no defenceless territories with weapons in their hands; they built no forts upon ground to which they had no right; nor polluted the purity of religion with the avarice of trade or the insolence of power".

At length, as the culmination of a series of political events, the time came when Christianity was awarded legal recognition in the Empire. The next thing was that, through the favour of Constantine, it was accorded rights and privileges hitherto reserved to those who professed paganism. Sunday was recognized as a public holiday, and grants were made to churches and clergy. This Emperor felt it necessary, at first, to temporize somewhat; and he continued to exercise the office of Pontifex Maximus, and to keep the coinage on which his image appeared embellished with pagan emblems. When, however, he became master of the whole Empire, he began to build Christian places of worship, using the materials of the temples for the purpose. Still, even at this period, he was careful to reassure those who still adhered to the old way of worship. Unfortunately, his sons introduced into Christendom the dangerous weapon of force. Constans made it a capital offence to offer sacrifice in private houses. Later, the revenues of the temples were confiscated; until eventually, in 391, an edict prohibited under penalties the ancient worship, the frequenting of the temples and the veneration of the idols. Theodosius II excluded all pagans from public offices. Under Honorius, the Sibylline Books were burnt. Paganism was now on its death-bed and lingered only in Sardinia and Corsica. We can well understand the astonishment which this sudden change-over created in the Christian body. Eusebius, the historian of the period, describes it as a spectacle the like of which was never witnessed on earth; and he speaks of the Roman Emperors spitting in the face of the idols, trampling the profane rites under foot, and laughing at the musty errors handed down by their forefathers.

All the same, error yielded slowly and contrived to maintain some sort of hold upon the people by means of their age-long customs and superstitions. At the beginning of the fifth century, a procession in honour of Cybele, organized annually for the protection of the harvest, took place at Autun in Gaul. When the Emperor Honorius came to Rome in 404, the shrines of Jupiter and Minerva still crowned the Capitol, the sacred geese were still being fed, and the pagan festivals and games were still marked on the calendars. In the same century, Pope Leo deplores the fact that even Christian society is still tainted by paganism; and we are told that, at this time, worshippers entering St. Peter's were accustomed to mount the platform in order to make their obeisance to the rising sun (*Sol Invictus*). The invectives of popes and preachers were powerless against a blood-lust that kept the gladiatorial shows going until the fifth century. The monk Telemachus, who dared to make a public protest against this sadistic institution, was seized and cut to pieces by order of the prefect Alipius who, presumably, was a Christian. When pilgrims from the north arrived in the Eternal City in the eighth century, they were amazed to find its public squares still profaned by pagan dances.

VI

THE ISLES OF THE NORTH

TO those familiar with Cardinal Newman's writings, the title of this chapter will recall the historial sketch in which he describes the irruption of the Barbarians into the Empire, and the momentous enterprises of which it was the inspiration. This calamity, in fact, proved to be a decisive turning-point, not only in the history of Europe, but in that of the apostolate as well. The missionary movement to which it gave birth continued without interruption for seven centuries, and created the spiritual world known as Christendom. From now on, in place of sporadic and individual efforts, we have an evangelistic crusade that is concerted and organized. From now on, we are largely done with obscurity and conjecture; everything tends to become plainer and plainer, until the missions make a proper front-door entry into literature.

It is not necessary, at this point, to consider these invading hordes in detail, since the story belongs, for the most part, to the European mainland. Having described the havoc they wrought, Newman continues: "In such distress, islands have commonly been the retreat to which the hopes of humanity have been conveyed"; and he represents the Church as looking round for one such retreat, in which the hope of the future might be lodged, and finding it at last. "High up in the north lay two sister islands, happy in soil and climate, ample in size and far away from foreign foes. Here lay the solution of the problem. These two islands were destined to be the store-house of the past and the birth-place of the future."

It is quite impossible to discover when, how or by whom Christianity was introduced into Britain. Here again we meet with the familiar determination to claim an apostolic origin for the Church there. No fewer than five Apostles have been put forward as claimants for the distinction. Of the Glastonbury legends, it has been well said that, although they are not facts, their existence is a great fact. That is to say, they bear witness to the importance of Glastonbury which, of all the greater churches of England, is the only one which authorizes us to lay aside the name of England and fall back upon that of Britain.

Legends and traditions apart, it is certain that there were Christians in the country at an early date; and the presumption is that they arrived from Gaul, or even from Rome, in the come-and-go that went on between these centres and our island during the occupation. The wife of the proconsul Plautius—the military governor who did more than anyone to consolidate the conquest—and the wife of the Senator Pudens are believed to have been Christians. The first of these was a Roman and the second a British lady. And, indeed, there is evidence that the knowledge of the Gospel was not confined to foreigners. The proto-martyr St. Alban was a citizen of Verulam who had been converted through the good offices of a priest to whom he had offered hospitality. At the same time, two other natives, Julius and Aaron, suffered death for the faith at Caerleon-upon-Usk. Such Christianity as there was was not even confined to Roman subjects, for there are traces of its having reached the independent tribes of the north about this period. In the documents, the churches of Spain, Gaul and Britain are mentioned together, and three British bishops sat at the Council of Arles held in 314.

Before the close of this century, armed bands from Ireland had begun to occupy the western shores of Great Britain, some north of the Clyde and in Galloway and Cumberland, others along the Welsh coast and down to the English channel. It is claimed that when St. Patrick visited Britain in 428 he instructed these colonists. It is claimed again that many of these converted Britons assisted him in the task of bringing Ireland into the fold. The hermit Brenach is mentioned as being the first Irish saint known to have devoted himself to missionary work in Britain. This was in the middle of the fifth century. He concentrated on Wales and—so it is alleged— won over the pagan chieftain Brecan after whom Brecknockshire takes its name. Many of his countrymen followed his example and laboured to spread the Gospel through the Principality, some of them even penetrating into the interior. During the same period a succession of Irish missionaries diffused themselves over the western part of Cornwall.

From these apostles are derived a considerable number

of the place-names of that district: St. Ives, St. Piran, St. Buryan, St. Levan, St. Feock, St. Ruan, and so on. By the time the Romans abandoned Britain, the whole of the western area, Wales and Cornwall, had been Christianized with the exception of a few remote localities inhabited by the aboriginal tribes.

With the Anglo-Saxons came disaster; first to the southern parts of the island, and next to the northern. Between 569 and 586 the defenders of the faith were finally cast out beyond the Severn, while bands of the usurpers drove the Picts back to the far side of the Tweed and founded the future kingdoms of Mercia and Northumbria. The two last bishops of the conquered territory, those of London and York, fled to the mountains of Wales. Paganism was again rampant in all that was already beginning to call itself England. Only in the extreme west and north, where the enemy could not penetrate, did the British Church still maintain its footing and its succession of priests and bishops. These latter refused to co-operate with Augustine in the work of evangelizing the Anglo-Saxons; but, by the ninth century, the antagonism of the ancient British Church had so far weakened that it accepted the jurisdiction of Canterbury.

It is admitted that, although Ireland is indebted to St. Patrick for its faith, there were some Christians in that country when he landed, and some pagans still left when he died. In 430 Palladius, a native of Britain and a bishop, was sent by Pope Celestine "to the Scots believing in Christ". If, as appears almost certain, these Scots were those of the mother country, such a delegation would imply that numbers of the faithful had, somehow or other, accumulated there, thanks doubtless to the intercourse then existing between the island and the Continent.

We cannot deny that poetic fancy has taken many liberties with the Saint's biography, but there seems no reason for doubting the traditional account of his early years. He was sixteen when the raiders snatched him away and carried him to Ulster, where he served as a slave until he was twenty-two. With the recovery of his liberty came the call that determined his future career.

In dreams thou heard'st thy distant children cry,
To bid thee, holy one of God, draw nigh
Lest all the Gaelic clans but live to die.

It was to the schools of Gaul that he turned for his education, and St. Martin of Tours was probably his preceptor. On being consecrated under the name of Patritius, he set out with a number of associates and landed near Bray, in 432. There are good grounds for believing that he was specially commissioned by Pope Celestine. His first move was to the north where he converted his old master together with the bulk of the people of Ulster. It was here that he erected his first church at Saul in Downpatrick. At Slane he lighted the Easter fire and then went north again into Leitrim. Having founded another church on the borders of Cavan, he crossed the Shannon and abode in Connaught for seven years. Here he made his first purchase of land. The *Confessions* tell us that he was always careful to pay his way, and to return gifts laid on the altar, in order that his motives might never be in doubt. It was at this time that, in Roscommon, he instructed and baptized two of the king's daughters, to which incident is ascribed the tradition concerning the shamrock. Passing to Mayo, he climbed the slope of Croagh Patrick and banished the reptiles; and then traversed Donegal, Tyrone, North Antrim, South Down, Monaghan, Meath, Munster, and Leinster. By now he felt the need of headquarters. On applying to a chieftain, he was given the hill of Macha, now Armagh (Ardmacha), on which he built a church which has ever since been the seat of the primacy. He lived to be very old and died in Saul.

This apostolate exhibits a number of striking features all of which are an eloquent testimony to the energy and sagacity of this front-rank missionary. At no time in his life was he content to sit back and leave the hard work to his subordinates. He addressed himself in the first place to the kings and chieftains, but only with a view to getting at the masses who were ever his particular concern. With the future always before his eyes, he set up cloisters and schools, saw to the training up of native priests, three thousand of whom he is said to have ordained, and pieced together, bit by bit, the whole machinery of a prosperous and durable ecclesiastical economy. Where possible, he respected the *status quo*, disturbing little in the civil and political institutions of the country. Having purged the laws of their paganism, he allowed them to stand. He showed shrewdness and humanity in appointing to clerical offices the native brehons and bards, poets and historians, as being the traditional guides of the people. Himself of no great learning, his first clergy were only expected to be able to read and write; but in 450 he founded a seminary at Armagh. Druidism fought him relentlessly, employing in the fight all the devices usually resorted to in such cases—lies, trickery and even assassination; but he conquered them, as Elias conquered the priests of Baal, by out-wondering their wonders. The simplicity which characterized him all the way through passed into his followers and successors, to become the conspicuous badge of the Irish missionary everywhere. For belongings, his clergy had a catechism, a missal, a ritual and a copy of the Scriptures; while his bishops had, in addition, a bell, a chalice, a crozier and a leather satchel containing a few books.

Just as the primitive Church conformed, in her organization, to the organization of the Roman Empire, so the communities which St. Patrick established were modelled on the sept or clan; in each district the bishop was the spiritual chieftain, and lived surrounded by his clergy and the members of his flock, men, women and children. Celtic monasticism is considered to have developed of its own accord, to have owed nothing either to Egypt or Gaul, and a great deal to the clan system. The collective life of the clan did not suit everybody. Before long, the more individual members of the religious tribe broke away and went off to live as solitaries. They were joined by others, until their hermitages grew into monasteries. But this monasticism betrayed its origin to this extent that the nephew or cousin of the founder usually succeeded to the office of superior. The first eleven abbots of Iona were of the same stock as Columba.

Of the saint's method of instructing we are given a sample in the records. To the questions asked by the pagan daughters of the King, Patrick gave a concise explanation of the nature and attributes of God, garnished with those nature-images so favoured by the Celtic missionary—by St. Columba, for instance—as being calculated to appeal to a poetic people accustomed to the instruction of the Druids and the songs of the bards. Heaven, earth, sea, rivers, sun, moon, stars, mountains, valleys, the wells of the deserts and the islands of the ocean— all are the works of His hands who gives life to all and breath to all. And, with Him, His Son is co-eternal and co-equal, and the Spirit proceeds from both. Father, Son and Holy Ghost are Three in One (as the Shamrock is). "To this God I desire to unite you by faith." And when the girls had asked to be shown how this faith was to be acquired, he instructed them still farther and ended with a series of questions.

"Do you believe that by baptism you put off the sin inherited from the first parents?"

They answered: "We believe."

"Do you believe in penance after sin?"

"We believe."

"Do you believe in life after death and in the resurrection on the Day of Judgement?"

"We believe."

"Do you believe in the unity of the Church?"

"We believe."

Then they were baptized and were clothed in white garments.

Although the name Scotland came into use only in the eleventh century, when the Scots of the west began to exercise sovereignty over the whole country, we shall use the denomination here to describe the forest territory in the centre known as Caledonia, as well as the adjacent districts occupied, on one side by the northern, on the other by the southern Picts. Until the fourth century, all is uncertain regarding the introduction of Christianity into these regions, although the stereotyped surmises are not lacking.

Ninian the Apostle of the southern Picts is "the first authentic personage that meets us in the succession of Scottish missionaries." During the Roman occupation, the Firths of Clyde and Forth, connected together by an earthen rampart, formed the northern boundary of Britain. The first of these

Firths, together with the wall, formed also the northern boundary of the kingdom of Strathclyde, whose capital was Dumbarton and which, after the Romans left, extended its sway as far as the river Mersey. During the struggle with the legions, and more especially after the legions had departed, there was a considerable infiltration of Irish into this territory, so much so that part of the district beyond the Solway became known as Gallgaedhel or Galloway. The tradition claiming Strathclyde as the birthplace of St. Patrick is a thousand years old; although it appears to be generally admitted that his parents hailed from Celtic Gaul. And Galloway was the birthplace of Ninian.

He studied in Rome, was consecrated there and returned to his birthplace about 402. Venerable Bede says that he drew out of the darkness of idolatry all those inhabiting the region south of the Grampians, and that he established his see at Whithorn, so named from the church of white stone which he built there—a style of building to which the North Britons were unaccustomed. A recent survey revealed the existence of some sixty churches dedicated to this saint in Scotland. Before his death, Ninian divided the territory he had evangelized into districts, placing a missionary in each. The fame of Whithorn brought many men and women from Ireland, whose sanctity and apostolic labours have left marks upon the land of their adoption.

In the next century, three brothers crossed over from Ireland and took possession of a piece of territory which was destined to develop into the Kingdom of Scotland. This territory, which roughly corresponded to the present county of Argyll, received the name of Dalraida. Christians themselves, they were accompanied by missionaries who spread the faith in this district, and are said to have made a settlement of some kind on the island of Iona. One of their number, St. Modan, has been described as the Apostle of Argyllshire.

Some twenty years before Columba's coming, Kentigern or Mungo had begun work in Strathclyde. The tradition is that the house he was born in stood in what is now St. Enoch's Square in Glasgow, Enoch being Thenog, the saint's mother, in whose honour a chapel was erected there. Kentigern, who was consecrated in 540, was a typical missionary bishop of the time. Clad in a goat-skin over which he wore an alb and a stole, he travelled everywhere on foot, from the shores of Loch Lomond to the shores of Windermere. His pastoral staff was a wooden cudgel with a curved top. Eight churches in Cumberland still bear his name.

On the eve of Pentecost, 563, Columba landed with twelve monks at the southern extremity of the island now known as Iona. This domain, which was about six square miles in extent, and was made over to him by his relative the King of Dalraida, was to become, next to Armagh, the greatest centre of Gaelic Christianity, the spiritual capital of Caledonia, a school from which missionaries went out in every direction to preach the Gospel, and the coveted burial-ground of some seventy kings and princes.

What exactly did the apostolate of Columba amount to? To him must be attributed the conversion of the northern Picts. After some years of preparation, he set out for Inverness in the company of St. Comgall and St. Canice or Kenneth. Admission to the royal residence was at first refused, but one sign of the cross made the gates fly open of their own accord, and this miracle induced the king to listen to the preacher. This conversion inaugurated a missionary movement that spread to the whole of Caledonia.

Over and above, there is some reason to credit his influence with the foundation of certain great monastic missionary centres between the Forth and the Tweed. On the other side of the Forth, the round towers of Abernethy, Brechin and Dunblane proclaim their Irish origin and their connection with the Abbot of Iona, who was the pioneer of Irish efforts in those districts. Nor can it be forgotten that St. Aidan, who, more than any other, saved the Christian situation in Northumbria, was of the monastic family of Columba. Another disciple of his, St. Machar, fixed his episcopal residence at Old Aberdeen; while there is a tradition that monks from Iona brought the Christian faith to the Orkneys in the lifetime of the saint. St. Cuthbert did not begin the evangelization of Lothian until some forty years after Columba's death. But the abbey of Old Melrose which was the base of his operations was a Celtic foundation.

Apart from the work he did for religion, Columba deserves

honourable mention on the score of the humanitarian services which he combined with it. These are now taken for granted as an integral part of foreign missionary enterprise everywhere, but in this department he was something of a pioneer, at any rate by reason of the extent to which he carried such ministrations.

At the beginning of the eighth century, the Scottish Church began to lose its essentially monastic character. In 717 the Columban monks who resisted the adoption of the Roman Easter were expelled by the Pictish king. Their places were taken by the Culdees who had formed themselves into communities after being solitaries pure and simple, and by the secular clergy who were introduced into the country at this time. The primatial see of the kingdom was fixed first at Dunkeld, then at Abernethy and, eventually, at St. Andrews. Meanwhile, the Norsemen and Danes had overrun the west and devastated Columba's foundation at Iona. They appear to have adhered to their paganism until the eleventh century, when the Orkneys and Hebrides were re-Christianized through the good offices of St. Margaret and her husband Malcolm.

VII

A.D.597 AND AFTER

OF St. Augustine's mission and the events succeeding it, we possess more abundant information than of any missionary undertakings so far, not accepting those of St. Paul. Almost all the gaps that tantalize us in the history of the apostolate during the first four or five centuries are here filled in. Almost all the lesser things—the gossipy or domestic details—that account for so much of the interest taken in missionary enterprises, are here told and well told. There are a hundred and one matters connected with the first Apostles and their immediate successors concerning which we wonder and wonder, and are left wondering. But few if any mysteries have survived the exhaustive record we possess of the conversion of the Anglo-Saxons.

For all this we are indebted to the careful and patient pages of the Venerable Bede. He was not the first ecclesiastical historian, but he is one of the best; better perhaps than Eusebius, who was well-up in Eastern affairs but badly informed about those of the West; certainly better than Gregory of Tours who was too partial to sensationalism, and too heedless of ordinary events. It is only necessary to read Bede's account of Pope Gregory's questionary concerning the slave-boys, to realize what a "feel" he had for the niceties, and how shrewd his appreciation was of the curiosity of his readers. The boys, he says, had white skins, beautiful faces and very fine hair. He puts the whole story before us, puns and all; and he begins by protesting that he is not at all disposed "to pass over in silence" an account handed down by the tradition of our forefathers. It is just this unwillingness of his to pass things over in silence that qualifies him for the work he undertakes, and leaves posterity so much in his debt.

When Gregory encountered the Angles or "Angels" in the Roman market place, he was only a simple Benedictine monk, and his first idea was to go to England and attempt its conversion in person. When he heard that it was proposed to elevate him to the papacy, he escaped from the Eternal City by hiding himself in the wicker basket of a carrier. Having

been brought back, however, and put in charge of the whole
Church, he lost no time in promoting his great scheme. He
was not content to call for volunteers and then dismiss them
to their posts with a blessing. His published *Letters* reveal the
born organizer who leaves nothing to chance, and who stands
by the work he has initiated until its success is practically
assured. During the first critical years, he was prompt and
ready with his advice, steering Augustine through his
problems and perplexities.

Of the monks whom he chose to accompany Augustine, the
names of only four are known. Having equipped the expedition
with everything needful, Gregory proceeded to get out the
passports. There are several of these extant, and each takes the
form of a personal letter addressed to the rulers of the kingdoms through which the forty are to pass on their way to
the coast of Gaul.

"To Brunehault Queen of the Franks—Your Christian
Majesty is so well known to us that we by no means doubt of
your goodness, etc., etc. Will Your Excellency, then, con-
descend to consider Augustine, the servant of God and the
bearer of this, as commended to you in all things, and to
bestow on him the favour of your protection? And, in order to
render your recompense complete, will you furnish him with a
safe conduct on his way to the English people? So may God
grant you, here and hereafter, to rejoice with His saints."

It is largely owing to these letters that the route followed by
the missionaries through France can be traced. Leaving
Rome in the summer of 596, they probably went by sea to
Marseilles and then on foot to Aix. Here, it seems, they
encountered the first set-back in the shape of reports and
rumours as to the savagery of their prospective converts. No
doubt, the dreams of the more timid were disturbed by
terrible nightmares in which they could hear the Anglo-
Saxons sharpening their knives and see them starting to heat
up their cauldrons. Leaving his companions at Lérins,
Augustine returned to Rome for instructions, which were to
the effect that there must be no turning back. Eventually the
party moved forward in earnest; from Lérins to Aix again,
then to Arles, Vienne, Châlons, Autun, Sens, Tours, Anjou,
and so to some point of embarkation on the English channel.

It was probably in the Spring of 597 that the missionaries, increased now to the number of forty by the addition of interpreters taken up in Gaul, set foot on English soil. Thanet was a considerable island in those days and its insular character was more clearly defined than now. The channel which divides it from the mainland was then about a quarter of a mile in breadth. The normal thing for vessels on their way to London from the Continent was to enter the channel at Richborough and come out into the estuary of the Thames. But if the ship were bound for Kent, it would anchor at Ebbsfleet which now lies on the present road from Ramsgate to Sandwich. The spot was long venerated by our forefathers, and the stone supposed to have served as a foot-rest was preserved in the Chapel of St. Augustine's monastery at Canterbury.

At that date, Ethelbert was ruling over Kent. His wife Bertha belonged to the royal family of the Franks and was a Christian; to her Augustine presented a letter of introduction from the thoughtful Gregory. In his first interview with the missionaries the king was conciliatory yet cautious. Neither he nor his subjects could be expected to adopt the new religion without knowing what they were doing. Meanwhile they were welcome. Canterbury would be assigned to them as a residence and they might preach and make as many converts as they pleased. Proceeding, then, to Canterbury, Augustine took possession of a small church dedicated to St. Martin and, here, on the feast of Pentecost in the same year, Ethelbert was baptized. Before long ten thousand persons are said to have followed his example. It was Gregory's idea that, in the event of success, the English primacy should be established in London; but, since Canterbury was Ethelbert's capital, that city was chosen instead; and, in due course, Augustine, now consecrated, became the first Archbishop of Canterbury and Metropolitan of all England. Ethelbert himself was destined to be venerated as a saint by a grateful posterity, and until the Reformation a lamp was kept burning at his shrine in the Cathedral.

Before the end of the century most of the Jutes of Kent had been converted and, a little later, it was found necessary to erect a bishopric in London and at Rochester, while good progress was made in Essex. The timely marriage of the King of Northumbria to a Christian princess brought Paulinus to York where Coifi, the pagan high-priest, made his famous declaration, and followed it up by profaning the temple and the idols. Edwin was baptized and a goodly portion of his subjects followed his example. Soon after this, Felix the Burgundian won over East Anglia and Birinus began to evangelize Wessex. There were temporary reverses, and serious ones, especially in the north where paganism under Penda fought hard. Here, however, help came from an unexpected quarter, and brought upon the scene one who was to take second place after Augustine among the apostles of this country.

It was in 635 that Aidan set out from Iona for the royal residence of King Oswald. Left free to settle in any place between the Firth of Forth and the Humber, he chose the humble island of Lindisfarne, later known—and with obvious justice—as Holy Island. Although little religious attention has been paid to it in modern times, this unpretentious sanctuary has not lost its claim to be what Alcuin styled it, the most venerable spot in all Britain. Aidan was assisted by missionaries from Ireland; but, at an early date, he followed St. Patrick's example and trained up a native priesthood. He himself laboured for sixteen years, penetrating the wildest districts of his vast diocese and entering the houses of the poor as well as the rich. It is said that he never allowed a traveller or a tramp to pass by on the road without endeavouring to convert him. He preached in the open air, in fields or on the beach at Lindisfarne where Oswald acted as his interpreter. Holy Island sent missionaries out into the remote parts of the kingdom, St. Cedd to Essex, and St. Chad to Mercia; while St. Wilfrid the apostle of the South Saxons and St. Cuthbert, who consolidated the Christian position in the North, both served their apprenticeship in this place.

In 655 Woden made his last stand as far as England was concerned. Penda's reign was one long battle with the new religion and, in this year, he made his final bid in the vicinity of Leeds. Victory was on the side of the cross. The river over which the Mercians fled was swollen by the rains; it swept away the remnants of their army. Penda was killed, and the cause of the ancient gods was lost for ever.

This, then, is the bald outline of an enterprise which was brought to a successful conclusion within the space of eighty years, by means of the continual exertions of missionaries from Rome, Gaul and Iona; seconded, towards the end, by the services of natives, and in defiance of the opinion that the foundation of the faith must be cemented with the blood of martyrs. It brings into view, besides, the new technique already operating on the Continent; for, as Lingard remarks, "we shall look in vain for a missionary who ventured to preach in opposition to the civil power. The despondency of the bishops of Kent and Essex, after the death of their patrons, proves how much they depended on the smile or frown of the monarch; his favour assured, his opposition prevented success."

The Christianizing of England was, from first to last, the work of monks and, for a considerable time, the ecclesiastical life of the country was directed from the monasteries (minsters). Where the Celtic system prevailed, even the bishop was subordinate to the abbot. The parochial system, as we know it, was a thing of slow growth and developed out of the private chaplaincies attached to the estates of the great landowners. To the prevalence of these in England has been ascribed the presentation system, by which the right to appoint the incumbent was vested in the lay patron. By the end of the Anglo-Saxon period, the dioceses had increased to seventeen and every township had its parish priest.

VIII

THE BARBARIANS

IT now becomes necessary to retrace our steps—chronologic-
ally speaking—in order to review the mighty events going
forward on the mainland of Europe, events which, by a
mysterious dispensation of providence, culminated in the
conversion of the whole of our continent. To connect them
up with what has gone before, we may note that St. Patrick
was alive when Alaric entered Italy and sacked Rome, and
that he passed to his reward exactly fifteen years before
Odoacer or Ottokar, the chieftain of the Heruli, effected the
downfall of the Empire of the West.

In the ancient civilized world, the term Barbarian had a
precise meaning. St. Paul uses it to describe a person whose
language differs from his own, and that is its uniform meaning
in the New Testament. To the Greeks, all non-Greeks were
Barbarians, whether savage or not; and to the Romans, all
outside the pale of the Empire. Even in modern times,
treaties drawn up with the Chinese government used to
contain stipulations to the effect that the term was not to be
applied to Europeans in Chinese state-documents.

At the time of the great invasions, these Barbarians were
congregated in two major groups. On the north-east of the
Empire, in an area bounded (roughly) by the Carpathian and
Ural mountains, were the Huns, the Alani, the Heruli, the
Gepidae, the Ostrogoths (Eastern Goths), the Visigoths
(Western Goths), the Bulgarians and the Avars. The territory
lying between the Rhine and the North Sea and Baltic was
occupied by the Angles, the Saxons, the Burgundians, the
Vandals, the Lombards, the Suevi, the Alemanni and the
Franks. Although the Goths had been troubling the Empire
for some years, they did not make any serious inroad into it
until 375. Other invasions by similar races and tribes
followed, and resulted in the overthrow of the old order.

There is no need to particularize the successive moves and
counter-moves which culminated in this tremendous tragedy.
"As great Caesar fell, not under one but under twenty
strokes; so it was only by many a cleaving, many a shattering

50

blow that the existing fabric to which Caesar—more than any other—had given name and form was battered down." Although, at first, these outsiders had no intention of ruining either the Empire or the Christian Church, subsequent events proved too strong for them.

The various races or nations tended to ally themselves, the one with the other, or to quarrel among themselves; with the result that some were merged in their stronger neighbours, and some were liquidated altogether. As far as the scope of this sketch is concerned, this circumstance helps to simplify an otherwise extremely complicated situation. The Huns, who really started the trouble, having invaded Gaul and Italy and suffered defeat, appear to vanish without leaving any definite trace behind them. The same may be said of the Alani and the Gepidae. The Heruli eventually settled in the neighbourhood of Jutland from which they were expelled by the Danes; their subsequent fate also is unknown. The Avars were defeated by Charlemagne and later absorbed by the Moravians and Magyars. The Vandals subjected the Christians of Spain and Africa to a bitter persecution, but their complete disappearance from the scene coincides with their defeat by Justinian in 534. Incidentally, the faith never properly recovered in Africa and was extinguished altogether when the Mohammedans came.

At first and for long all was confusion. During their tentative raids into Roman territory, before the real trouble started, some of the Barbarians had become acquainted with the Christian faith. We know, for instance, that there was a Visigothic bishop present at the Council of Nicaea, held in 325, at which time or soon after, that nation appears to have had some sort of hierarchy and certainly a number of monastic foundations. We hear tell of Christians being taken prisoner by the Goths and carrying on an apostolate among their captors.

The most famous of these was Ulfilas (Little Wolf), a Cappadocian who was carried captive during a raid which the Goths made into Asia Minor. Being sent as a hostage to Constantinople, he was educated and consecrated a bishop. Returning to Dacia, the territory occupied by the Goths (roughly corresponding to Rumania with a piece of Hungary

thrown in), he laboured for forty years, and converted so
many that he is known as the Apostle of the Goths. He
translated the Bible into their language, a task demanding, as
a preliminary, the invention of a special alphabet. We say the
Bible, although the Books of Kings are missing from his version.
It has been suggested that this omission was deliberate,
since Ulfilas thought the Goths were warlike enough as it
was, and needed no Biblical or other encouragement. This
supposition, however, ignores the fact that he did include the
Book of Genesis in which the militant energies of Abraham are
set out in very uncompromising terms. This Bible is the
oldest extant literary monument of the ancient Teutonic
language and is "of priceless value in the history of human
speech".

But what Ulfilas gave to his converts was the Arian or semi-
Arian form of Christianity; so that when, later, they carried all
before them, they spread this heresy through Gaul and Spain
And history has much the same tale to tell of the other
Barbarian bodies, the Franks being a notable exception.

When the fifth century was drawing to a close, the condition
of the Christian Church was anything but encouraging. In the
whole of what had been the domain of the Roman Empire,
there was not a single ruler to be found who was not either a
pagan or a heretic. Some of the kingdoms founded by the
invaders were already showing signs of a promising future,
but none of them adhered to the orthodox faith. The Gospel
won through and triumphed for all that. Here again a great
secular instrument was placed in the hands of the Church in
the shape of the ascendancy of the Franks; a formidable
contributory factor being the speedy and triumphant conversion of Great Britain and Ireland, which provided Christianity with a recruiting ground for missionaries, at a time
when the need of these was wellnigh desperate.

Fortunately, as it turned out, a fairly large part of Gaul
passed into the hands of the Franks soon after the Western
Empire fell in 476. Having crossed the Rhine, a succession of
victories carried them as far as the Seine and, eventually,
to the Pyrenees. They not only occupied the country, but they
were able to defend it against the Alemanni, Saxons, Slavs
and Avars who might have made it their prey. When Clovis

had been baptized, his subjects were in a fair way to being Christianized because, at that time, subjects followed their ruler. Their real conversion was a slow process, especially among those of them who were settled in Belgium which was still very pagan at heart as late as the eighth century; but things were tending in a Christian direction all the time. Many evils and abuses are associated with the reign of the Merovingians; rulers and people were often, and in many ways, but sorry Christians. Still, they were always amenable to good influences and, in fact, the Irishman St. Columbanus, together with his twelve companions, effected a radical reform of the whole nation. From the Christian point of view, it was of capital importance that they alone of all the Barbarian hordes never became entangled in the heresy of Arius.

To those who criticized Clovis—and there was that in his life that deserved severe criticism—St. Remigius used to say: "Much must be forgiven to one who has been the saviour of the provinces and the defender of the faith". Legend has tended to obscure his character, but he stands out as an able statesman in an age when statesmanship was at a discount In the end, the whole of Europe came under the influence of his political ideas. His father, although a pagan, was on friendly terms with the bishops of Gaul who co-operated with him, and did a good deal to further his aims. On his accession, he received a message of congratulation from the prelate who later baptized him. Certainly, as far as the Church was concerned, he earned the title of The New Constantine. In conquering Gaul, his dynasty restored life to the peasantry and made it the backbone of the nation; and this partly accounts for the liberality which it extended to the bishops and monastic bodies, who created and maintained flourishing agricultural centres up and down the land. What the Franks under Charlemagne did to spread the Gospel through Europe is a commonplace of history.

The writings of St. Gregory of Tours are the chief historical authority for this period, and he has furnished posterity with a detailed account of how Clovis came to be baptized. From this account we learn what manner of men these rugged warriors were; and the sort of arguments that appealed to their warlike imaginations. Clotilde, his Catholic wife, reasoned in vain

5

with her husband who could not be persuaded to believe until a war broke out with the Alemanni. Then, when he found that the old gods were leaving him in the lurch, he turned to Jesus Christ and promised to believe should His help be forthcoming. He and three thousand of his soldiers were baptized at the same time.

The chrism used for this baptism, so it was believed, was conveyed from heaven by a dove. The vessel or *ampoulle* is preserved at Rheims, and was used at the consecration of every French king from Philip Augustus (1180) to Charles X (1824).

As for the dominant races and nations who survived the great invasions, their career belongs to the general history of Europe. Having devastated Greece, the Visigoths led by Alaric sacked Rome in 410. Insecurity compelled them to found a new kingdom in Gaul and Spain. The Franks drove them out of Gaul, but they contrived to maintain themselves in the Peninsula. Towards the end of the sixth century their king was converted, and during the next hundred years the Catholic faith spread throughout their kingdom. The Suevi settled in the north-west of Spain, were Arians at first and then Catholics, and became united with their Visigothic conquerors. Theodoric, the Ostrogoth, entered Italy soon after the chief of the Heruli had dethroned the last of the Western Emperors. He unseated Odoacer and ruled in his stead. An Arian, he left the Church alone at first, but before the end of his reign he began an active persecution interrupted by his death. Justinian destroyed the dynasty and made Italy a province of the Eastern Empire ruled by Exarchs at Ravenna. About this time, the Lombards came upon the scene and conquered the whole of the northern part of Italy, with disastrous consequences to the Church. Peace and prosperity only came with the conversion of their ruler Agilulf through the influence of his Catholic queen. Under King Grimoald, the Lombards were converted, although they continued to be a source of trouble to the popes. Charlemagne put an end to their rule in 774. Early on, the Burgundians had settled on the left bank of the Rhine. Catholics at first, they were corrupted by the Arianism they found when they invaded Gaul. Their king Sigismund, however, was a

Catholic and on his accession his subjects began to return to the orthodox faith. Soon after the Burgundian power was destroyed by the Franks. The Alemanni, whose whereabouts are identified with the present-day Württemberg, Alsace and north Switzerland, were gradually won over after their defeat by Clovis. What happened to the Angles, the Saxons and the odds and ends of Jutes and Frisians who occupied England, we have already seen.

IX

THE COMING OF THE MONKS

CHRISTENDOM was for so long identified with the European continent that we are apt to forget how slow and how gradual were the steps by which this important spiritual conquest was achieved. In spite of Charlemagne's determined and almost ruthless energy, he did not live to see one half of Europe won over, even in the most nominal form. When he died in 814, practically nothing had been accomplished in Bulgaria, Bohemia, Russia, Poland, Prussia, Lithuania and the Scandinavian peninsula. We can say that, when the great maritime discoveries were inaugurated by Prince Henry of Portugal (The Navigator), nothing farther remained to be done in Europe; but we are only just able to say it. Henry was born in 1394, and Lithuania only came within sight of conversion in 1386.

Oddly enough those whom God raised up to accomplish this formidable task were bodies of men whose original founders and leaders had rather frowned on the idea of their assuming pastoral responsibilities of any kind. Even those Church authorities who were most favourably disposed towards monasticism would not allow the monk to preach. This aloofness, however, did not last, for there are isolated instances of Egyptian solitaries quitting the desert in order to attempt the evangelization of foreign parts. Before long, the services of these monastics were in demand everywhere, especially for that sort of work. The number of priests in their ranks steadily increased, and many became bishops. The majority of the Fathers and Doctors of the later Church issued from the cloister; and, from about the fifth century onwards, missionary enterprise began to be monopolized by monks.

Spreading from East to West, and having gained a firm footing in and around the city of Rome, the new way of life soon extended itself over Italy. A solitary named Fulgentius quitted the Thebaid and built a monastery in Sardinia. The Vandal persecution was instrumental in driving many monks out of Africa into Spain, where they continued and extended their sphere of operations. Eusebius of Vercelli established monks in his cathedral—an example which in places was destined to become the rule—and these, as we have seen, became the nucleus of a kind of missionary congregation. The first monastery in Gaul was St. Martin's foundation at Ligugé near Poitiers; while Lérins was, for a century, the monastic metropolis of the West. Each of these was a nursery of missionary bishops and priests. It is generally agreed that a large number of the cities and towns of France originated in monastic enclosures, and some of these were established at this time. The influence the monks exercised over the Barbarian invaders was considerable, and we read of grants of land being made by these even while they were still pagans. Celtic monasticism, as we have seen, developed of its own accord; while England received it in its Benedictine form, along with the mission of St. Augustine.

Speaking of the spread of Christianity in the face of the weight and multiplicity of the obstacles confronting it, Cardinal Newman remarks that no social movement can come up to it; it is a divine and miraculous work which we soon cease to admire in order to adore. "But", he says, "there is more in it than its own greatness to contemplate; it is so great as to be prolific of greatness." He is referring to a phenomenon of Christian history an outstanding example of which belongs to this period, the proselytizing impulse, namely, which suddenly, and as though by magic, can take possession of those who themselves are but recent converts to the faith.

While the Continent was still swarming with the Barbarian invaders, the children of St. Patrick drew from their conversion a zeal and energy which flung them into battle with the heathenism threatening the Christian world. It was in the remote churches of Ireland and the Scottish Highlands that the beacon was kindled which, in the words of Alcuin, "caused the light of truth to shine to many parts of the earth". Bands of Celtic monks, whose immediate ancestors had been pagans, crowded to the shores of Europe. Their missionary work extended from the Orkneys to the Thames, from the sources of the Rhine to the shores of the Channel, from the Seine to the Scheldt; while groups of them specialized in navigation, and braved the unknown in order to carry the Gospel message to the Faroë Isles and distant Iceland.

The Irish missionaries were conspicuous everywhere for the simplicity of their character and the asceticism of their private life. They possessed neither gold nor silver, and what alms they received from the rich was transferred to the hands of the poor. They entered the towns and villages only to preach and administer the sacraments, and they were so detached and mortified that they accepted lands for the erection of monasteries only under compulsion. Thus has Venerable Bede described the bishops and priests of Northumbria, for all that he was so displeased with their custom of celebrating Easter.

As a rule, they travelled in bands with no baggage beyond a short pastoral staff made of wood for the most part, a wallet for provisions, a leather bottle containing milk or water, and a case for the service books. For short journeys they used their own small coracles or, where possible, the monastic galleys. A whole fleet of these was assembled at Iona, manned and navigated by the monks, seventy of whom were told-off for this duty. At that date, communication between Ireland and Gaul was quite frequent, and French merchants carried their wines and other wares as far as the great monastic settlement of Clonmacnoise. Even in those days, it was almost an understood thing that "monks never pay", and shipmasters often took them either for nothing or for a small fee. As a rule, they landed at one of the ports lying along the mouth of the Loire, or at one of the harbours on the coast of Flanders. Having paid their respects to the tomb of St. Martin at Tours or that of St. Hilary at Poitiers, they would cross France to the frontiers of heathendom.

Before long, these "soldiers of Christ", as they loved to call themselves, were reproducing in the heart of Europe the scenes that had been enacted under the oaks of Derry or in seagirt Iona. Having gathered their willow-switches and brushwood, built their huts with a chapel and round tower at the side, and arranged their farm buildings, they settled down to their life of prayer, study and work. Presently, the peasantry would begin to listen to their instructions. This is what happened at Luxeuil which in course of time became the missionary capital of Gaul and sent out its colonies into

Burgundy, the Upper Rhine, the Loire valley, the Ile-de-France, Champagne and Ponthieu.

Even at the risk of being tiresome, some mention must be made of the individual missionaries and their spheres of activity. At quite an early date, flourishing Christian centres had existed in the territory lying between the Danube and the Rhine; but these were mostly swept away during the invasions, so that the work of evangelization had to begin all over again. The pioneer of the revival seems to have been the Irishman Fridolin who became a monk in the monastery of St. Hilary at Poitiers. Before settling on an island in the Rhine, he traversed Baden, Württemberg, Alsace and north Switzerland—the domain of the Alemanni—earning for himself the nickname of "The Traveller". His work among the Alemanni was continued by St. Gall, the disciple of the renowned Columbanus, the Apostle of the Burgundians of the Vosges. Another Irishman, St. Lebwin, crossed over to Flanders, and laboured there until his martyrdom near Alost in Brabant. In Thuringia, the beginnings of the faith are identified with St. Killian, and in Carinthia, with St. Virgilius or Feargal, who became Archbishop of Salzburg. St. Findan spent twenty-seven years at Schaffhausen on the Rhine, and St. Fursey laboured for years in the diocese of Paris. St. Briach, St. Samson, St. Winwaloe and St. Paul de Leon are associated with the first traditions of Christianity in Brittany. St. Colman laboured in the neighbourhood of Vienna and is honoured as one of the martyr-patrons of Austria. St. Vulgan evangelized the district round Arras, Saints Turninus and Foillan worked together in the Netherlands, St. Disibod gave his name to the town of Disenberg near Bingen on the Rhine, St. Alto founded an abbey near Augsburg. These are only a few of the names of those the traces of whose labours are still to be found scattered up and down Europe. Even in Italy itself, no fewer than thirty churches are dedicated to St. Columbanus. These memorials bear witness to the generous return Ireland made to the Continent for the gift of its faith and civilization.

As for the Anglo-Saxons, in addition to the spiritual incentive operating in converts, they had a patriotic one, inasmuch as the vast regions of ancient Germany were inhabited by their own kith and kin. The first to lead his countrymen into this apostolate seems to have been St. Wilfrid, the Northumbrian, whose preaching converted large numbers of the Frisians (Low Germans) who inhabited a considerable part of Holland and Hanover. Another Lindisfarne monk, Egbert, migrated to Ireland and trained several bands of missionaries for work in this very region. With Willibrord at their head, eleven of these entered Frisia in 691 and preached there and among the neighbouring tribes as far as Denmark. Willibrord fixed his see at Utrecht and was assisted by several of his countrymen; by Swithbert, for example, who evangelized part of the right bank of the Rhine, and by Adalbert, who laboured in the northern part of Holland. The brothers Ewald attempted the then impossible task of converting the old Saxons living in north Germany— the most cruel and most incorrigible of all the Germanic tribes—and were martyred for their pains. The Batavi, who dwelt on the island formed by the Rhine and the Wahl, owed their conversion to Werenfrid who died at Arnheim. Wiro, Plechelm and Otger devoted themselves to the inhabitants of Gueldres or Gelderland.

But the most famous of all these Anglo-Saxons was Winfrid, born at Crediton in Devonshire, and later known as St. Boniface, *the* Apostle of Germany. He ranks among the greatest missionaries of all time, not only on account of the extent of his conquests and the importance of his commissions, but also by reason of the organizing genius which he brought to bear upon the work of evangelization. Unless the writer is mistaken, he was the originator and sponsor of a number of enterprises which have since become recognized features of foreign missionary work everywhere.

As soon as he was consecrated (by Gregory II) regionary bishop of all the Germanies, he addressed to the bishops and abbots of England a circular letter designed to foster vocations among their subjects. The result was that a large number of would-be missionaries crossed the sea and placed themselves at his disposal. This letter painted in lively colours the situation and needs of the mission in Germany, so that it has some right to be regarded as the forerunner of the famous *Relations* which the discovery of the new world brought into being, and which were themselves the precursors of our modern Annals and missionary magazines. Boniface believed in the apostolate of the pen and, like St. Francis Xavier, was an indefatigable correspondent. The letters that passed to and fro between himself and his native land are among the literary treasures of that far-off period. For his missions, he solicits alms as well as prayers; and we gather from the replies he received that many gifts in kind were forthcoming from the nuns—an altar cloth, the Acts of the Martyrs, a copy of the Scriptures, as well as an offering of fifty sols, which may possibly have been gold coins.

Another thing that Boniface did was to take steps to create a native missionary clergy, an obvious precaution which, in later ages, was to be sadly neglected. With this object in view, he erected several monasteries, and insisted that his colleagues should do the same in their several districts. This measure justified itself in a triumphant manner from the very start. A small child was entrusted to the saint and educated in one of his abbeys. His name was Sturmius or Sturmi. After his ordination, he was sent to evangelize the Saxons, and to choose the site of what became the central abbey of Germany, the monastery of Fulda, founded in 744. Placed under papal protection, this missionary centre continued to diffuse the light of culture and piety long after Lindisfarne, Jarrow and even Canterbury itself had been ravaged by the Danes. Sturmi went to Monte Cassino to train, and returned—the first German-born Benedictine—to rule over Fulda, whose abbots were princes of the empire and primates of all the abbots of Gaul and Germany. For centuries its monks carried the Gospel message to the shores of the Baltic and beyond.

Thanks to the ancient *Life* of St. Sturmi, we happen to know something of the course of instruction which those preparing for missionary work were required to undergo. He himself had to commit to memory the whole of the Psalms, besides divers religious readings, and had to have a sound knowledge of the Scriptures, especially of the four Gospels.

Boniface even took the bold step of inviting women to participate in the work of the missions. He wrote to the Abbess of Wimborne, in Dorset, who had some five hundred nuns in her charge. She despatched a large number of these to Germany, where they were later joined by a number of English ladies equally desirous of devoting their lives to this service. They opened and directed schools for the education of German girls, and they appear to have carried on a certain amount of medical missionary work at the same time. These Anglo-Saxon women established several abbeys in Germany some at least of whose subjects must have been natives. For the rest, Boniface evangelized Bavaria, Hesse, Friesland, Franconia and Thuringia. In his old age he was martyred along with fifty-two of his companions.

These Anglo-Saxon missionaries, almost without exception, belonged to the Order of St. Benedict which, at this critical time, not only lent a powerful impulse to the monastic movement, but also gave to the apostolate a more definite unity and plan. At the time of Benedict's death, in 550, the only European countries that had been properly Christianized were Ireland and, to a lesser extent, Italy, Spain and Gaul. The remaining nations were converted during the next half dozen centuries or so, and converted either wholly or in part through the energy of his sons.

What Boniface did at Fulda is a type of what the Benedictines did everywhere. With practised eye they sought out the proper site for their monastic home, saw that it occupied a central position with reference to the tribes amongst whom they proposed to labour, that it possessed a fertile soil, and was near some friendly water-course. These points secured, the word was given, the trees were felled, the forest was cleared, the monastic buildings rose. "The voices of prayer and praise awoke unwonted echoes in the forest glades." The brethren were never idle. While some educated the young, others copied manuscripts or transcribed a gospel. Others, again, cultivated the soil, guided the plough, erected the water-mill, opened the mind; and, thus, "the Benedictines presented to the eyes of men the Kingdom of Christ as that of One who had redeemed the bodies no less than the souls of men."

X

ONE THOUSAND YEARS AFTER PENTECOST

BY the middle of the eleventh century the conversion of Europe had been practically—if nominally—completed. The scope of this book forbids anything like a detailed account of how this was effected, of how the multitude of pagan races were, at one and the same time, Christianized and welded together to form the nations figuring in the atlases of modern times. The general picture of the situation is, more or less, as follows.

Having subdued the Saxons, after a bitter struggle, Charlemagne established eight bishoprics amongst them. At that time they were located in north Germany, so that their defeat opened the road for the evangelization of the Scandinavian nations. Denmark was the first of them to receive the conqueror's attention; but, although it was very soon reduced to submission, the country remained pagan until well into the eleventh century, when the German emperor persuaded its ruler to embrace the faith. In Jutland, three bishoprics were set up and the king was converted some fifty or sixty years before.

It was not until the end of the ninth century that Norway began to have a single ruler. Haakon, the son of its first king, became a Christian and endeavoured to bring his people into line. Little progress was made until the reign of Olaf the Saint who, a few years later, actively promoted the spread of the Gospel among his unwilling subjects. The first effort to convert Sweden was made by the Frank St. Ansgar and, after him, by his successor in the archbishopric of Hamburg. But internal troubles undid the work accomplished by these two, and some years were to pass before anything further was attempted. Olaf of Sweden was baptized in 1008 and this gave the missionaries their chance; but, although there were wholesale conversions, the bulk of the population remained pagan at heart for a considerable period.

Meanwhile, Rollo the Norwegian Viking, with his band of pirates, had sailed up the Seine and taken Rouen. He accepted Christianity in 912 and began to rule over that part of France henceforth called Normandy.

Icelandic historians ascribe the first discovery and evangelization of their island to the Irish sea-faring monks. The
Norwegians colonized it in 861 and, although they were
pagans at that time, they came into contact with Christianity
on their journeys to and fro. The first known missionary to
Iceland was commissioned by King Olaf of Norway in 996.
We next hear of two native converts returning to labour among
their compatriots, and of a native bishop being appointed in
1056. Greenland was another Norwegian colony, planted by
Eric the Red (who gave it its name) towards the end of the
tenth century. Eric's son visited Norway and was induced to
become a Christian by Olaf the First. Missionaries accompanied him when he returned and, with their arrival, the
Cross had reached the farthest known point in the north-west
of our continent. Whatever was done at this time in Greenland
seems to have been done for the colonists. From the beginning
of the fifteenth century, no bishop visited the country,
and the Christians lapsed into the paganism of the
aboriginal Eskimos. Contact with Christendom was not
resumed until 1735 when a Lutheran pastor undertook to
found a mission amongst them.

Frankish prowess or influence also smoothed the way for
the conversion of the Slavs, the Indo-Germanic race that
took possession of the whole of eastern Europe during the
sixth and seventh centuries. Of these, the Croats, having
migrated from Russia, settled in part of ancient Pannonia,
Dalmatia and Illyria. Charlemagne occupied northern
Croatia and, the chief of the nation having been converted,
the population was brought into the fold through the preaching
of SS. Cyril and Methodius. Moravia also was a dependency
of the Frankish empire and this, too, came under the influence
of the preaching of the two brothers, the latter of whom
achieved great success by the liberal use he made of the
vernacular language. He had permission to celebrate the
Liturgy in Slavonic. Cyril converted the Khazars, a curious
people living between the Caspian and the Dneiper who, for a
time, professed Judaism; some maintain that the modern Jews
of southern Russia are their descendants. St. Cyril also
directed his energies to the Bulgarians, who in the seventh

century entered the territory formerly known as Thrace and Moesia. King Bogoris was so moved by his eloquence and by the sight of a picture of the Last Judgement that he asked for baptism. This was in 864.

Bohemia, called after the Celtic Boii, was overrun by the Marcomanni whose queen, Fritgil, applied to St. Ambrose for instruction in the faith. The Czechs came two centuries later and were compelled to pay tribute to Charlemagne. Fourteen of their chiefs were baptized at Ratisbon in 846. This nation produced a famous missionary in the person of St. Adalbert (in Czech, Voitech), Bishop of Prague, who preached the Gospel in Poland. Carinthia, part of the ancient Noricum, was converted in the eight century owing to its connection with Bavaria. The Duke of Poland was baptized in 966 through the persuasions of his Catholic wife Dubrawka, and the people followed his example. The bishopric of Posen was established in the year 1000. The Wends who dwelt between the Elbe and the Oder, in a territory now included in Saxony and Prussia, became Christians, of a sort, after their conquest by the Saxons in the tenth century. The Serbs had been compelled to accept baptism by the Emperor Heraclius as early as 620, but they fell away and were brought back again only at the end of the ninth century. The Magyars invaded what is now Hungary about the same time, established paganism in it, were defeated by Otto the Great in 955, and formally accepted Christianity under Stephen about the year 1000. Vladimir entered the fold in 987 and his conversion marked the beginning—a slow and painful beginning—of that of his Russian subjects.

From now on little remained to be done except to instruct the converts and habituate them to the ways of the Christian life. In places, however, paganism was still defiant. Prussia did not give in until it had been properly Germanized, and that only happened in the latter part of the Middle Ages. Livonia was evangelized towards the end of the twelfth century by an Augustinian Canon named Meinhard. Esthonia accepted the Gospel some thirty years later. The conversion of Finland was delayed until the end of the thirteenth century. Christianity was proclaimed the state religion of Lithuania in 1386, but little or nothing had been done as yet to evangelize the people. As for Lapland, although attempts to convert it were made during the early Middle Ages, things remained very unsatisfactory right down to the sixteenth century, when the people were enrolled as members of the Orthodox Church. But the faith never secured a real footing amongst the Lapps, and the story of their evangelization belongs to our own times.

Although this rapid review takes account of between twenty and thirty different states or kingdoms, each with a separate missionary story to tell, all the stories are strangely alike in their main features. In almost every case, the initiative lay with the civil power; and this circumstance was at once the strength and the weakness of the apostolate during this decisive period. Charlemagne's reign alone contributed, to a greater extent than that of any historical personage, to the build-up of the religious fortunes of our continent. He made a Christian Europe possible, first, by driving the Moors back beyond the Ebro; next, by breaking up the centres of lawlessness of which the Continent was then mainly composed; and, finally, by establishing and bequeathing to posterity a rule of statesmanship which was adopted by all who took the future of Europe seriously.

A few instances may now be elaborated in order to a better understanding of the kind of political framework within which the missionaries were compelled to do their work.

Actuated by a desire to put an end to what he regarded as a moral and political menace, Charlemagne launched against the Saxons a series of campaigns lasting thirty years. Shortly before their final defeat, he drew up a formulary obliging them to accept baptism on pain of death, and to pay tithes for the support of the Church. When they lost their last battle soon after, their chief Wittekind "acknowledged the God of Charles to be greater than Woden", and was baptized in the presence of the Emperor himself.

One result of Charlemagne's policy is amusingly reported by the Monk of St. Gall in his account of the *Deeds of Charlemagne*. In order that his readers may understand what some of the Northmen really thought of their baptism, he proposes to tell a story which, he says, has been handed down "by our grandfathers". The story is to the effect that, after the death of Charlemagne, the Northmen continued to send ambassadors

to the court of his son Louis, just as they had done formerly.
On these occasions the customary procedure was followed.
They were asked if they were willing to be baptized, and,
having answered in the affirmative, the rite followed as a
matter of course, the new converts receiving the gift of a white
baptismal robe, as well as other presents. One year, fifty came
together and, since new robes were not available, odds and
ends of cloth were cut up and made into garments. When the
oldest of the candidates came to be clothed in his make-shift
outfit, he was very wroth. Turning to the Emperor, he said
to him: ' This is the twentieth time I have been baptized here,
and never before was I treated in this shabby fashion.
Formerly I was given a brand-new outfit, and now you offer
me a sack fit only for a swineherd."

A resistance almost as determined as that of the Saxons
was put up by other races. Prussia, for instance, fought
as long and as hard as any. Here the beginnings of the
state and of Christianity are connected with the bloody
struggle by means of which the Baltic territory between the
Elbe and Memel was wrested from the Slavs and won for
Germany and the Church. This struggle lasted for seventy
years. The first missionaries met with a violent death. To
avenge these wrongs, the military order called the Brothers of
the Sword had been founded, but their efforts met with
very little success. The Teutonic Knights were thereupon sent
in with an army of German crusaders. The Knights then
turned upon the Lithuanians who were of the same stock as
the Prussians, and for nearly a hundred years maintained an
ineffectual struggle against them. At length, in 1251, one of
their princes sought baptism, for purely political reasons, and
was crowned king. But the Lithuanians refused to follow his
example and, in fact, the new king went back to paganism ten
years later. It was not until the marriage of Jagello to Blessed
Hedwig of Poland that paganism in Lithuania began to lose
ground. This was in 1386.

It was Olaf the Saint who really consolidated the Christian
religion in Norway. He succeeded his father in 1015, at a time
when a portion of his kingdom was partitioned between the
Danes and Swedes. These districts he reconquered, after which
he exerted himself to win over his realm to Christ, for he

himself was already a Christian. He brought over from England a number of pious and learned priests one of whom, Grimkel, was chosen Bishop of Nidaros, his capital. In order to stamp out idolatry, Olaf travelled in person from town to town exhorting his subjects. Unfortunately he was not content with exhortation and he used force without compunction. The sagas have a good deal to say about his severity; but this, as Boyesen says in his *History of Norway*, "was in accordance with the practice of the times, and as a politician Olaf sincerely believed that the only hopes for law and order in Norway lay in the acceptance of the faith". He put down pagan practices with a ruthless hand. At Drontheim, he found a tribe still persisting in the old festivals and sacrifices; by his order, their chief was slain and many of his followers killed or outlawed. In the end, resentment against his policies and methods produced a war which cost him his life.

All the same, by Norwegians generally Olaf has always been regarded not only as their apostle, but as the champion of their country's unity and independence. Bishop Grimkel had a chapel built on the spot (now Drontheim) where the King fell, and on the return of his son Magnus to power, the cult of St. Olaf became widespread. Later the chapel was replaced by a cathedral which became for Scandinavia what Canterbury was for England.

Another ruler whose missionary zeal cost him his life was St. Olaf of Sweden. His conversion was not followed by that of his subjects and, in the year 950, they put him to death for refusing to conduct the customary pagan sacrifices. This is said to have happened on the spot where the city of Stockholm now stands.

While Olaf was striving, with more zeal than discretion, to make a one and independent Christian Norway out of rival groups of pagan Northmen, St. Stephen was carrying out a similar policy at the other extremity of Europe. The Magyars entered what is now known as Hungary in the latter part of the ninth century. They were pagans, but had come across Christianity in their raids into Italy and France. Still, they steadfastly refused to accept the religion of those whose territory they had usurped. At last, one of their leaders called Géza consented to be baptized, for political reasons, along with some of the nobles. His son Stephen, however, was carefully brought up by his Christian mother; and, when he succeeded his father, he embarked upon a crusade—part military, part religious—the object of which was to make the Magyars into a nation. The opposition he encountered was so formidable that when, at last, the decisive battle came to be fought, Stephen's forces were completely outnumbered. Still, with the assistance of the German Knights whom he had brought in, he gained the victory. The missionaries then went to work in earnest and made many conversions, accompanied and assisted by Stephen himself. It was claimed that he had obtained from Pope Sylvester II the title of Apostolic King and Legate, with the right to have the cross of a primate carried before him, but the document conferring these extraordinary privileges has been proved to be a forgery.

It is admitted that Stephen acted in an arbitrary manner, to say the least, that he connived at the coercive measures used to propagate the Gospel, that he was violent in his manner of suppressing ancient customs and superstitions and that, while his laws prohibited any except ecclesiastics from remaining single, they forbade marriages between Christians and pagans. All this led to great exasperations and involved the king in recurring uprisings and revolts. He was no sooner dead than a part of the nation reverted to heathenism. In 1046 there was a rebellion against the Catholic faith which resulted in the martyrdom of the Bishop of Buda who was thrown into the Danube.

In his book, *The Russian Church*, Brian Chaniov asserts that it is a grave distortion of truth to affirm, as certain Orthodox historians do, that Christianity was welcomed throughout Russia with open arms. As far as can be gathered, the first missionary, St. Adalbert, a monk of Trèves, entered that country in compliance with a request which Queen Olga made to the Emperor Otto. This was in 962. But the people were so far from being in agreement with their sovereign on this point, that Adalbert narrowly escaped death and had to flee back to Germany. According to the Russian Chronicles, Vladimir, Olga's grandson, championed the Christian cause after his baptism. He commanded the pagan idols to be chopped in pieces and burnt; after which, at Kiev, he made

6

the following proclamation: "Whosoever tomorrow, rich or poor, mendicant or artisan, does not come to the river to be baptized, will be as an alien to me." When the people heard the words, they came joyfully saying: "If this faith were not good, the prince and the boyars would not have adopted it." When they were baptized, the people returned to their homes and Vladimir rejoiced that he and his people knew God. He ordered that churches and priests should be established in all the towns, and that the people should be baptized throughout all the towns and villages.

But certain facts are brought forward by Chaniov which give a very different picture. The people of Novgorod, especially, strongly resisted the introduction of the new religion into their midst. That their opposition was overcome by force is confirmed by certain popular sayings still current among them. These are to the effect that their ancestors were baptized not with water, but with fire and steel. The planting of the faith in Rostov was accompanied by great brutalities. This district was only partly pacified, for the people drove out the first two bishops and put the third to death. Almost everywhere, in fact, the work of the missionaries was hampered by discontents, risings and reprisals. In the north and east, the Finnish population resisted for a long period.

XI

FOOTNOTE TO THIS PERIOD

UNLESS some attempt be made to read between the lines, the foregoing summary will be sure to lead us astray. Compressions are apt to be unsatisfactory; and the compression that space has compelled us to make results in the elimination of nearly everything except the uninspiring political machinery employed in the evangelization of the Western nations. This machinery played its part in the conversion of our country; but, had England's story been subjected to a similar compression, Ethelbert, Oswald and company would have monopolized the record, to the exclusion of all its richest and most relevant ingredients. The conversion of Europe was brought about, effectually and in the long run, not by the Charlemagnes, Olafs and Stephens, but by the patient, and largely anonymous, day-to-day exertions of ordinary priests, some few of whose names have managed to survive.

The compression is not too fair even to the secular rulers themselves, since, in order to squeeze them into the picture, nearly everything has had to be taken from them except their swords. Yet, Charlemagne was a statesman, and a Christian, rather than a soldier. At any rate, he was no mere soldier who fights for fighting's sake. Of his fifty-three campaigns, only about a dozen were undertaken for purely political motives. If he compelled his opponents to choose between war and baptism, that was because he was sincerely convinced that Christianity alone could bring unity and order into the chronic confusion and chaos. And this conviction of his was shared by all the enlightened princes of that age.

Certainly, during this epoch so fateful for Europe, converts were admitted into the fold by national and, apparently, indiscriminate baptisms; and, once the chief had made his submission, in many cases the submission of his people followed as a matter of course. But we must not judge those rude and difficult times by our own, or forget the peculiar nature of the tie binding rulers and ruled together. As one writer says: "No preparatory dispensation had made monotheism natural to these heathens or taught them—line upon line—those elementary truths which appear so easy of apprehension to us who have lived in an atmosphere permeated with their influence." These European converts were not "proselytes of the gate", but infants in knowledge and civilization: and they were admitted to infant baptism by teachers often themselves imperfectly educated, but who were "faithful in a few things" they did know, and so in time were made "rulers over many".

Vladimir warned the Russians that those of them who refused to be christened would henceforth be as aliens in his eyes; a remark which throws all the light we need on that particular aspect of the situation. That there were abuses, we may well believe, apart from the Monk of St. Gall's lively story. But it was always regarded as a profanation to baptize those who were likely to be brought up as, or to continue to be, pagans. The Code of Justinian was very severe on those adults who, for worldly reasons, went through the formality of being baptized (*pro forma*). Orphans and foundlings were admitted to this sacrament, being presented at the font by the Christian women who undertook to see to their upbringing (perhaps the origin of sponsors); but it does not appear that this was ever done in the case of young children who were, and were likely to remain, outside the fold.

Fortunately we are in a position to know that the instruction, when it came, was thorough and systematic if simple. Preeminently objective in character, it concentrated chiefly on the outstanding facts in the life of our Lord, especially on the signs and wonders He wrought, since these appealed strongly to the heathen's imagination. Thus, Augustine, having caused an image of the Crucified to be displayed before his Kentish audience and having explained the Incarnation, described how the star appeared over Bethlehem, how Jesus walked on the sea, calmed the storm, rose from the dead and ascended into heaven.

The fifteen sermons which St. Boniface left behind make it evident that he required far more from his converts than a merely formal profession of the faith. Much, too, can be learnt from the famous discourse of St. Eligius of Noyon, himself a missionary of experience. He propounds the general question, "Who is the good Christian?" and then he sets forth not only the duties appertaining to piety and religious observances, but above all to the obligations of the moral law. Unscrupulous controversialists garbled this discourse in such a way as to make it appear that the saint laid all the stress on churchmanship, but Cardinal Newman made short work of their trickery.

In his correspondence with Charlemagne, Alcuin the Englishman also deals with this subject. He says that, in teaching the heathen, the order should be followed which St. Augustine lays down in his treatise *On Instructing the Ignorant*. Having been diligently exercised in the great verities of the faith, the Trinity and Incarnation, the converts are to be baptized, with the proviso that their faith is to be deepened and expanded by means of public preaching, until they grow to the full stature of the perfect Christian.

In approaching the heathen, in the first instance, the missionaries usually endeavoured to expose the absurdity of their mythologies. Gregory of Tours, for example, is at pains to report the conversations Clotilde had with Clovis when she was trying to convert him; and we may believe that the line she took was more or less the general line at that time. "These gods of yours," she says in effect, "are nought, for how can stone and wood do anything for themselves, far less for others?"

It was by such arguments that Oswy of Northumbria endeavoured to convert Sigebert, King of Essex. From the adoration of such trumpery gods, he bids his royal brother turn to the Creator and Ruler of all things who is invisible, omnipotent and eternal. It will be recalled that, when Paulinus was attempting the conversion of Northumbria, the pagan priest Coifi delivered himself of sentiments very much to the same effect. The great thing was to impugn the *power* of these false deities, to discredit them in the eyes of the populace, and then to insist upon the omnipotence, the wisdom and the providence of the true God. This explains how, again and again, in different places, the apostolate starts off with the destruction of some idol. This was a challenge to the god in question; and, when it remained unanswered, the spectators drew the obvious conclusion that his powers had been very much overrated. The prevalent belief seems to have been that the god dwelt in his own idol or, at any rate, protected it, and Oswy reminds Sigebert of what, by that time, was undeniable, namely that many of these idols had been broken and trampled under foot without anyone being a whit the worse for it. The aforesaid Coifi followed up his comments with just this very challenge; Vladimir of Russia did much the same thing, and with the same object in view; and so did Boniface, following the example of his father in God, Benedict, who at Monte Cassino broke the idol and cut down the grove of Apollo.

A certain amount of temporizing had to be done for a time, and was even recommended, not with idolatry or wrong-doing, but with customs that, from time immemorial, formed a part of domestic and social life. The idols were to be destroyed, but the temples preserved and converted into churches; even the sacrifices of oxen were to be allowed, but transferred to Saints' Days. This was Pope Gregory's advice to Augustine, and he justified it on the plea that "he who aspires to the highest must ascend step by step and not at one bound". Daniel, Bishop of Winchester, wrote a letter to his friend St. Boniface couched in similar terms, namely, that customs not vicious in themselves ought to be preserved and given a Christian context. It is of interest to know that the formula of baptism used by Boniface and his associates required the candidate to renounce all connection with Woden and Thor. Before very long the civil power took practical steps to see that such connection was, in fact, renounced.

XII

THE COMING OF THE FRIARS

WHILE the spiritual subjugation of our continent was in full swing, Eastern Christianity was suffering a series of set-backs which culminated in its partial extinction in those widely-extended territories identified with its first and most triumphant successes. A new and, as it turned out, the most formidable enemy the Christian faith ever had, started up in Arabia during the reign of the Emperor Heraclius.

This was Mahomet or Mohammed, an illiterate man endowed by nature with a most compelling eloquence, a fanatical energy and remarkable political astuteness. When he was forty years of age, he believed himself to be the recipient of special revelations from God conveyed to him by the angel Gabriel. Threatened by the civil power, he fled from Mecca to Medina in 622 and, from being a religious reformer pure and simple, became a political adventurer as well. On the eve of the capture of Mecca, his birthplace, he wrote to the potentates of the world promising them security, provided they embraced the Islamic faith. As soon as he found that power was in his grasp, he set about preaching the necessity of spreading the Gospel by the sword.

To connect up this anti-Christian crusade with the events recorded in the preceeding chapters, we note that Mahomet made the famous flight, which is the beginning of the Mohammedan era, exactly twenty-five years after Augustine landed on the shore of Kent, and died (632) when the kingdom of the Merovingian Franks had nearly reached its widest extent.

After his death, Mohammedanism conceived the idea of becoming a world-power and a universal religion, and with amazing rapidity set about putting its ambition into effect. Within the space of less than a century, Syria, Palestine, Mesopotamia, Egypt, North Africa and the south of Spain were annexed to the new empire. The Moslems even crossed the Pyrenees, but their defeat at Tours in 732 arrested their western conquests. In the eighth and ninth centuries, they conquered Persia, Afghanistan and a large part of India; and, in the twelfth, became the masters of all western Asia, Spain and even Sicily. In the next century they were conquered by the Mongols and Turks, but the victors adopted the religion of the vanquished and, in 1453, overthrew the Byzantine Empire. From Constantinople they threatened the German Empire, but were defeated under the walls of Vienna and driven back across the Danube in 1683. As it was, they overran the Balkan peninsula and were not expelled from it until modern times.

In all these territories, with the exception of Arabia, a kind of restricted tolerance was extended to the Christian inhabitants. In spite of this, and to a great extent owing to the disunion produced by the prevalent heresies, the faith suffered serious reverses in the East. The Mohammedan laws were calculated to encourage apostasy, and in this they succeeded only too well. In time, Christianity disappeared from northwest Africa, and the great community at Carthage became extinct in 1160. On the other hand, apostasy from Islamism was punished by death, and this constituted an almost insurmountable barrier to the missionaries who, in the Middle Ages, attempted to convert the Mussulmans. Islam is still *the* missionary problem. The followers of Mahomet account for about one-tenth of the population of the world.

The Mohammedan conquests meant that Europe was more or less hemmed in on its southern and south-eastern frontiers, so that for a long time nothing could be done to evangelize either Africa or the Far East. In the latter region, such missionary enterprise as there was was carried on by the Nestorians.

Those who adhered to the authority and teaching of Nestorius, the deposed Patriarch of Constantinople, were driven by the imperial edicts into Persia where they established themselves. Henceforth the history of Christianity among the Iranian race is practically their history. During the next two centuries, the Nestorian Church, which regarded Nestorius as a saint, developed to such a degree that it surpassed, in power and extent, any other national or autonomous Christian body. Its hierarchy of bishops ruled over flourishing communities in Assyria, Babylonia, Chaldea, Arabia, Media, Khorasan, Persia proper, Turkestan and the shores of the Persian Gulf. In course of time, its monks (who had probably never heard of the doctrinal errors of Nestorius) evangelized the islands of Socotra, Ceylon, the coasts of Malabar and even parts of China and Tartary.

In 1625, a monumental slab was discovered in China at a place called Si-ngan-fu. A Jesuit named Nicholas Trigault was then sent from Pekin to inspect and decipher what became known as the Nestorian Monument, the text of which is to the effect that a person called Olopen arrived from Ta Ts'in (Persia) at Ch'an-gnan in the ninth year of the period Changkwan (635). He was received by the minister of the Emperor and conducted to the royal palace. The Scriptures having been translated into Chinese, the Emperor became convinced of the truth of Olopen's religion and gave special orders for its propagation. The conclusion drawn is that the Olopen in question was a Nestorian monk, who travelled from Persia and was the pioneer of Christian missionary work in China.

Two circumstances combined to produce this remarkable diffusion, namely the rise of monasticism, and the fact that Persian commerce was largely concentrated in Nestorian hands. The Nestorian merchants opened up the East to the Nestorian missionaries, and in the eleventh century their monks succeeded in converting the chief of a Tartar tribe dwelling to the south of Lake Baikal, in what is now southern Siberia, together with the bulk of his subjects. He was a vassal of the Chinese Empire and was destined to become known to posterity as Prester John. Some of his successors adhered, at least nominally, to the Nestorian faith and, even after the last of these had been slain by Jenghiz Khan, their Christian subjects were not interfered with. Before long the Mogul conquest overran Persia; but the Nestorian Church escaped again, and their patriarch was now chosen from people having the same language and lineage as the conquerors. He was, in fact, a native of western China and ruled during the reign of seven Mogul kings, some of whom he baptized. For a time, it looked as though these kings would unite with the Christians of Europe in a combined offensive against the Mohammedan; but this hope proved to be illusory. What happened was that the Moguls turned to Mohammedanism, as being more suited to their style, and the Nestorian Church came to ruin. After Tamerlane (1370-1405) hardly a trace of Christianity was to be found east of the Kurdish mountains.

In the century preceding this final disaster, two monastic bodies were founded in the West whose subjects were almost to monopolize missionary work for several centuries, and to resume the apostolate in the Far East where the Nestorians had left off. These were the Mendicant Friars, belonging to the Order of St. Francis and of St. Dominic, who came into being almost simultaneously; the one in 1223 and the other in 1216, these being the dates of their official confirmation.

The Poor Man of Assisi himself was consumed with a missionary zeal that took in the entire universe. To this work his Rule devotes a special section. At the second General Chapter of his followers, he assigned a separate sphere of activity to each of his foremost disciples. These missions were all directed to the conversion of the Mussulmans, as was the one he assigned to himself. Of this latter, *The Fioretti* gives us a memorable picture.

Inspired by this example, the Franciscans have always devoted particular attention to the Holy Land. In the first century of their existence, missions sprang up there, as well as in Rumania, Greece and all the Balkan countries. They did something, too, in Lithuania in spite of the opposition of the Teutonic Knights who, for political reasons, wished to keep the population pagan. In the next century, thanks to their labours, the faith was extended in Bosnia, Serbia, Bulgaria, as well as in the afore-mentioned regions; and in 1309 the Caliph of Egypt, in a firman, gave them leave to reside in Jerusalem and in Bethlehem. Later the Holy Sepulchre and the Cenacle were bought from the Caliph and given to the Brethren; and the purchaser, Queen Sancia of Naples, established an endowment for the upkeep of twelve of their number.

Meanwhile several of the Founder's sons had made their way to Morocco under the leadership of Berard of Carbio who, besides being a persuasive preacher, was well versed in the Arabian tongue. They were apprehended on arrival and given a choice of renouncing their faith or suffering death. Berard thus became the first of the thousands who were to sacrifice their lives during subsequent centuries. The bodies of these protomartyrs were brought back to Portugal and given a public funeral, one spectator of which was he who—on this very account—attached himself to St. Francis and earned a world-wide reputation under the name of Anthony of Padua.

From this time onwards Franciscans continued to attempt the conversion of Libya, Algiers, Tunis and Morocco. Abyssinia was visited by the renowned John of Montecorvino about 1280, and a great number of his brethren followed up his attempts, many of whom suffered death. Ethiopia, in fact, has been identified with Franciscan missionaries for nearly seven hundred years. The Genoese vessels which made the circuit of Africa in 1291 had two Franciscans on board, and the same Friars accompanied Vasco da Gama when he doubled the Cape and discovered an ocean route to the East Indies. In a second expedition they went to Mozambique. At this time, a Franciscan preached the Gospel in Cape Verde, another was made Prefect Apostolic of Guinea (Liberia and the Gold Coast), from which a mission was dispatched to the Congo resulting in the conversion of one of its rulers.

The most remarkable Franciscan missionary of this period was Raymond Lull (*d.*1315) whose many-sided interests have wrapped his life in legend. He was by nature a poet; he was also a philosopher. But the thought uppermost in his mind was the conversion of infidels. At Palma, in the Balearic Islands, he founded the college of Miramar for Friars Minor who felt called to work for the conversion of Islam. Thirteen students were accepted at a time: they were taught Arabic, and care was taken to develop in them a psychological insight into the mentality of those whose conversion they were going to attempt. Convinced that the Crusades, in which there was political wire-pulling, no longer served any useful purpose, Lull wished to see in their place missionary activity, and the union of the Greek and Latin Churches. Like a gleam of light in the darkness, his project shone over the Holy Land. But Raymond was not content to direct operations from afar off. Having reached Africa and after toiling there for many years, he was stoned to death at Bougie on the Algerian Coast. During his last agony, so it is said, he repeated these words: "Beyond the curve of the sea which girds England,

France and Spain, there is another continent which we neither see nor know; it is a world ignorant of Jesus Christ." One of the listeners kept these words in his heart, and in his family they were handed down from one generation to another. His name was Stephen Columbus.

Side by side with these activities of the Franciscans ran those of the Dominicans, one of the most remarkable features of whose Order has been the versatility of its members. As prelates and simple ascetics, as philosophers and theologians, as artists and scientists, under every aspect of learning and religion, society has been indebted to St. Dominic's children. But it was essentially in an apostolic character that this new Order presented itself to the eyes of its contemporaries. St. Dominic himself is said to have converted 100,000 persons by his sermons alone. During the first centuries, the Friars Preachers exercised unceasing missionary activities within Christendom and beyond. The evangelization of Morocco was begun as early as 1225, and that of Tunis followed soon after. This mission was honoured by the activities of another Raymond, the Dominican one, since canonized, namely, Raymond of Pennafort. It was he who encouraged Thomas Aquinas to write his celebrated *Summa* against the Gentiles. In the north of Europe, the province of Dacia—where the Goths used to live—sent men as far as Greenland, while that of Poland extended its apostolate to Kiev, Dantzig and Ruthenia. From the province of Hungary, a missionary expedition was sent out in quest of the Hungarian pagans living on the banks of the Volga. The needs of Asia were catered for by a picked band known as Friars Pilgrims for Christ who, based on Constantinople, penetrated to Bagdad and India, to Armenia and Persia. The Order had fifty monasteries in Armenia within thirty years of its being founded. The Dominicans were also associated with the Franciscans in those part-diplomatic, part-missionary embassies despatched to the Far East by the medieval popes.

Better, perhaps, than any mere statistics, the story of St. Hyacinth's career will illustrate the energy that characterized this remarkable body of religious. He is styled the Apostle of the North and not without good reasons. He belonged to one of the most ancient families of Poland and joined the Order in the lifetime of St. Dominic. Having preached the Gospel in his native land, he passed over into Prussia and the countries lying near the Baltic and then went on to Denmark, Sweden and Norway. We next find him in the Ukraine, in Ruthenia, in Muscovy or Russia proper, among the Tartars and, it is said, in Tibet.

XIII

MISSIONARY EMBASSIES TO THE FAR EAST

DURING the lifetime of Francis and Dominic, momentous political events brought East and West together for the first time in recorded history. Jenghiz Khan, who died the year after St. Francis, had extended his conquests from one extremity of China to the other, into India and, eastwards, as far as Georgia. After his death, his mixed host of Mongol, Turk and Tartar warriors crossed Russia, overran Hungary and penetrated as far as Saxony, inflicting terrible hardships on the Christian population of those territories. The obvious thing to do was to open up negotiations with the representatives of this new and unpredictable power, with a view to its pacification and ultimate conversion. To these ends several missionary ambassadors, chosen from the ranks of the Mendicant Orders, were posted off to the Far East.

Of these, perhaps the most outstanding was the Franciscan Giovanni del Pian dei Carpini. He was one of the great missionaries of his time, and had laboured in Germany, Bohemia, Hungary, Poland, Norway, Denmark and Sweden. Although he was so stout that he could not walk but had to ride on a donkey, and although he was in his sixty-fourth year, he undertook to beard the Great Khan in his den. After a difficult journey across Russia, he and his associate reached the Mongolian encampment on the bank of the Volga. From thence they were escorted by soldiers to the royal residence at Karakoram, the ancient capital of Mongolia. This part of the journey, over two thousand miles in all, was attended by great hardships. They were just in time to witness the coronation of the new emperor, Kuyut, which took place in a huge tent and in the presence of four thousand ambassadors, some of whom had travelled thousands of miles.

The next on the scene was another Franciscan, John of Montecorvino, who was born in 1246, the very year in which Carpini's mission took place. For a time he worked as a foreign missionary among the Mongolian hordes then occupying Persia and threatening the West. While there, he heard that the Chinese emperor, Kúblái Khan, was not ill-disposed towards the Christian faith. At once, he went to Rome to make this fact known to Pope Nicholas IV. By this pontiff he was entrusted with a mission to Farther China where, at this period, Marco Polo still resided. He set out in 1289, accompanied by a Dominican friar and an Italian business man, and provided with letters to several eastern princes including Kúblái himself. His route lay through Georgia, Armenia and Persia, after which he sailed for India where he remained for over a year, preaching and baptizing. His Dominican companion having died, John journeyed into central Asia and China, on foot and alone, unable to make his confession, to receive news from Europe or to send messages home.

Having reached China, he found that Kúblái was dead and had been succeeded by Timurleng, or Tamerlane, a name-sake of the Turk who conquered Persia and liquidated the Nestorians. With this ruler he established a friendship from the start. In spite of the obstacles put in his way by the Nestorians, he settled down in Pekin and, before long, was able to build two churches one of which was next-door to the imperial palace. Among the converts he made was a Nestorian ruler, a vassal of the Great Khan, who is referred to by Marco Polo as being a descendant of Prester John. Having bought one hundred and fifty boys from their pagan parents, he formed them into a choir school, taught them Latin and Greek, and translated hymns and psalms for their use. He not only preached in Chinese, but he made a version of the Psalms and New Testament in that language. In 1307, Pope Clement V sent seven Franciscans with authority to consecrate John Archbishop of Pekin and all adjoining territories. Of the seven, four died on the way, but the three survivors duly carried out their commission. The new archbishop ruled for twenty years and, when he died, was honoured as a saint by Christian and pagan alike. It is of interest to note that he said Mass according to the Roman rite in the Chinese language.

There were other expeditions besides these. Four Dominican friars were sent to interview the general of the Mongol forces in Persia, in the year of Carpini's return. They were badly received and dismissed with a defiant letter addressed to the

Pope. St. Louis of France despatched the Franciscan William of Robruck to the court of Kuyuk's successor, with no better result. Worst of all, the religious foundations established in the Far East were short-lived. In spite of all the sacrifices involved, they never had a chance to consolidate themselves; so that, when the Spanish and Portuguese missionaries appeared in those lands in the sixteenth and seventeenth centuries, they found hardly a trace of the medieval communities. The people of Pekin did not even know that there ever had been Christians in their city. But, although they failed in their immediate object, the western travellers and missionaries did draw the attention of Europe to the existence and potentialities of the great nations dwelling on the shores of the eastern ocean. To these kingdoms they gave the name of Cathay, now heard in Europe for the first time. Such of them as survived to return home and tell the tale created an interest in and zeal for the conversion of those regions which later bore abundant fruit.

The Middle Ages, therefore, drew to a close in an atmosphere of despondency as far as the foreign missions were concerned. All at once, however, Portugal set her heart upon the sea and prepared to become a first-class maritime power. This unexpected development, which was to revolutionize apostolic enterprise, began with the capture, in 1415, of the Moorish stronghold of Ceuta opposite Gibraltar. Christendom attached so much importance to this new turn of affairs that the Pope confirmed to the King of Portugal all the territory his nationals should succeed in wresting from the Moors. Ceuta was made into a diocese, the first of the many sees destined to be erected in those pagan lands to which the Portuguese, from now on, set about carrying their faith and their flag. Prince Henry the Navigator organized a series of voyages which led to the rounding of the Cape of Good Hope. It was a good name for it, as far as the foreign missions were concerned, for it opened up sea-communications with the hitherto almost inaccessible Far East. Henry was chiefly responsible for the discovery of Madeira, the Azores and Senegal; and a number of his countrymen, famous in the annals of sea-faring, continued where he left off. Vasco da Gama crowned his achievements by disocvering Mozambique and sailing to the Malabar coast, where he entered into an alliance with the King of Calicut who later became a Christian. Thus was the way prepared for the dazzling missionary enterprises of the sixteenth century in which the Jesuits were to play so conspicuous a part. Spain took to the water about the same time and, from the start, considered it a duty to propagate the Christian religion in any place which she might annex and colonize.

In effect, Christendom was now on the eve of the greatest expansion in her long history; an undreamed-of expansion, since it had to do with a vast continent the existence of which was not suspected even when the approaches to it—its suburbs—had been actually occupied. As if to compensate her for the calamities which had fallen upon her in the homeland, the Church was to see her delegates going farther afield and achieving greater successes than at any period since the apostolic age.

XIV

IN THE WAKE OF COLUMBUS

THE discovery of the Western Hemisphere came, then, as the culmination of a series of expeditions which brought Portugal and Spain to the front as colonizing powers and patrons of foreign missionary undertakings. Columbus, who was a Genoese by birth, served his apprenticeship in Portuguese ships; and, when he made up his mind to try to reach Asia by sailing westwards, he naturally turned to Portugal for support. The refusal of the king threw him upon Spain with results that are known to everybody. Rivalry was inevitable and the disputants requested Pope Alexander VI to act as umpire. This he did and his Bull of Partition, issued one year after the discovery of America, appointed the meridian running one hundred leagues west of the Azores as the boundary line between the two, all territories west of the line going to the Spaniards and all to the east going to Portugal. By a later arrangement, Portugal secured Brazil which Pinzon and Cabral discovered between them.

Columbus made his historic landing on October 12th, 1492. A year later, at the instigation of the Pope, the Spanish sovereigns organized and despatched the first missionary body to visit the New World; as far, that is to say, as can be known for certain. This consisted of twelve Franciscans with a Benedictine named Boil in charge as Vicar Apostolic. When he reached Hispaniola (Haiti), he found that the first Mass in the New World had been offered up the year before in a rude shelter made of boughs. On this site, Boil built and consecrated a church—the mother church of the Americas.

This claim, of course, takes no account of the possibility that the services of religion were first performed in the Western Hemisphere by the Irish missionaries who are alleged to have made contact with it hundreds of years before. Nor does it take into account the less remote possibility that something of this sort was done when the Norwegians reached the American mainland, on the supposition, of course, that they did actually reach it. The Spaniards certainly came across some curious traditions current among the natives, particularly in Mexico.

What one writer describes as "a halo of rapture" invested these first missionary undertakings. The charts and atlases produced at the time were embellished with pictures showing the friars embarking on the ships, with the Blessed Virgin looking down from a sky on which was lettered the caption: *Mater Dei Monstravit Viam*; *The Mother of God Has Pointed The Way*. An inscription on the sails was to the effect that the world of the West was too small anyway: *Unus Non Sufficit Orbis*.

Throwing a kind of spotlight on the New World, we note that Cuba, visited on Columbus' second voyage, was conquered and occupied in 1511. Little was left to be done here since nearly all the aborigines were exterminated under the cruel administration of Fera Soto, the second governor. The diocese of Cuba was erected in 1518. The Island of Jamaica has much the same distressing story to tell. Visited by Columbus in 1494, and eventually occupied by the Spaniards, the natives were systematically wiped out; so that, until the African negroes began to be imported as slaves, the missionaries had little to do beyond catering for the spiritual needs of the colonists. Discovered by Magellan in 1521, Spanish sovereignty was established in the Philippines when Legaspi arrived from Mexico forty-three years later. He was accompanied by some Augustinians. The Dominican de Salazar arrived in 1581 and, from the beginning, espoused the cause of the wretched Filipinos with such fearlessness that he became known as the Las Casas of the Philippines. He was the first Archbishop of Manila.

The territory known as the United States of Columbia is noteworthy, because here it was that the first episcopal see on the American continent was set up in 1514. The Columbian city of Cartagena is associated with the name of St. Peter Claver; while in the Jesuit college of Bogota the first instruction in mathematics and physics was given to the natives of the newly discovered continent.

Between 1531 and 1534, Pizarro invaded and conquered the Inca territory which extended over more than one-half of the entire South American continent. During the next twenty

years, the work of the missionaries was thwarted by the
constant up-risings of the natives, rendered desperate by the
behaviour of the Spanish conquerors whose thirst for gold led
them to inflict unspeakable injustices upon the population.
St. Francis Solanus made a journey from Peru to the
Paraguayan Chàco preaching to the tribes in their own
dialects. The first Jesuits were sent to the country by St.
Francis Borgia in 1567. From Peru, the Gospel was brought
to Chile by Dominicans in 1541. The resistance of the
Araucanian Indians in southern Chile has no parallel in the
history of the Spanish conquests. For nearly two hundred
years, they defied the efforts of the soldiers and missionaries
alike.

The coast of Ecuador was first seen by Pizarro in 1525 but
the country was not permanently occupied until 1534. The
bishopric of Quito was set up ten years later. The Dominicans
laboured at this time among the Indian tribes bordering the
Amazon, and the Jesuits arrived in Quito in 1596. In the end,
the latter had thirty-three missionary settlements; but when
they were expelled, the Christian natives relapsed into
paganism. Sebastian Cabot made a settlement in the Plate
River in 1526 and the Spanish Franciscans founded the city
of Assuncion ten years later. The evangelization of the
Argentine (La Plata and Patagonia) did not properly begin
until the Jesuits came in 1586.

The first missionaries in Brazil were Franciscans and
secular priests, but in 1549 the Jesuits began to arrive, one
of whom Fr. Joseph Anchieta, is called the " Apostle of
Brazil". Penetrating into the interior, they reclaimed a great
number of cannibals whom they gathered into "Reductions".
Their work was constantly hampered by the Portuguese who
made continued efforts to enslave the native population. The
Franciscans followed the conquistadors into Paraguay soon
after 1536. The Jesuits took charge half a century later, and
established what has been described as "the noblest mission
ever formed since the days of the Apostles"; the "triumph of
humanity" according to Voltaire.

In little more than half a century, mission stations were
dotted over the face of the continent; from northern Mexico to
southern Chile, from the Atlantic to the Pacific; in Florida,

Alabama and Georgia. One hundred years of missionary work in South America was thus summarized by Ranke the German historian: "In the beginning of the seventeenth century", he writes, "there were five archbishoprics, twenty-seven bishoprics, four hundred monasteries and innumerable parishes. Magnificent cathedrals had arisen the most gorgeous of which, perhaps, was that of Los Angeles (in Chile). The Jesuits taught grammar and the liberal arts, and a theological seminary was connected with their college of San Ildefonso. All branches of theological study were taught in the Universities of Mexico and Lima. Meanwhile the Mendicant Orders had begun steadily to propagate Christianity all over the continent. Conquest gave place to missions, and missions gave birth to civilization. The monks (friars) taught the natives the arts of reading and singing, sowing and reaping, planting trees and building houses; and they, in return, were regarded with profound veneration and affection by the natives."

The missionaries themselves were in the first instance and for the most part drawn from the ranks of the two Mendicant Orders. The Augustinians played their part quite early on, as of course the Jesuits did at a later period. It seems to be generally agreed that, had it not been for the support and influence of the Franciscans and Dominicans, Columbus might never have set sail at all. The Franciscans, who were the first to celebrate the rites of religion in the new continent, traversed it from end to end, and left behind durable evidence of the share they had in its evangelization in the names of its cities and towns. As Padre Gemelli says: "While the conquerors thought of little else besides gold-mines and slaves, their eyes saw and sought for souls; while others introduced the latest weapons of war, they imported the latest agricultural implements and books; they did not send to Europe for fresh contingents of soldiers, but rather for artisans, doctors and schoolmasters."

The achievements of these religious men can be seen at their best in Mexico (New Spain) which was the most important of the Spanish conquests, comprising as it did all the territory of Central America, as well as California and Texas. A beginning was made, where the City of Mexico now stands, by gathering the children together for instruction. These were soon drafted into a school, the first institution of its kind to be erected in the New World. The Archbishop of Mexico reported, in 1551, that already more than a million Indians had been baptized by the Franciscans alone, the apparition of our Lady of Guadalupe noticeably affecting the flow of conversions. To Mexico belongs the further distinction of having possessed the first nuns seen in this hemisphere, and to the same friars the credit of establishing the first printing-press which opened its career with a work in Mexican and Spanish published in 1539. In little more than a century after their arrival, Mexico contained about two hundred Franciscan convents, to most of which a school was attached for the education of the native youths. Three colleges for higher education were opened in 1553, followed by the foundation of the University which received all the privileges and faculties of Salamanca, and had chairs of medicine and native languages.

It is admitted that the Mexicans were brought into the fold by mass-conversions. But they were not coerced. The Inquisition was established amongst them in 1534, and a year later a native chief was condemned to be burnt for ritual murder. After this, the natives were withdrawn from its jurisdiction, so that its activities were confined to Europeans and creoles. The method of mass-conversion was adopted everywhere in the beginning and, under the circumstances, was the only practical way of dealing with the people. Having been baptized, they were brought, and remained for good, under all the Christian influences that surrounded them.

Although a Dominican accompanied Columbus on his voyage in 1492, it is not until 1510 that we find the first regular mission in America opened by the Friars Preachers. It is said that, in that year, Father Bartholomew of Las Casas sang the first High Mass heard in the new territories. This was at Vega in the Antilles. The greater proportion of the first American bishops were chosen from the Order. Its members were the first ministers to arrive in Peru. After the conquest was achieved, one of the Dominicans who accompanied the conqueror from Spain was made Bishop of Cuzco with jurisdiction extending over all the dependent territories of the newly-annexed domain. It was not long before he was assassinated, a circumstance which illustrates the opposition the missionaries encountered on the part of the natives who, naturally enough, identified the Spanish clergy with the spoilers and oppressors of their nation. But in spite of the continual uprisings of the vanquished and the civil wars waged by the victors themselves, the work of conversion went steadily on and churches, monasteries and educational foundations sprang up everywhere. The Inquisition, of which the Dominicans were in charge, was not established in the colony until 1570, when a tribunal was erected in Lima whose writ ran as far as Chile on the one side and Buenos Aires on the other. But, by an express permission, the Indians were withdrawn from its jurisdiction and left to be dealt with by the ordinary courts.

Jerome de Loaysa, the first Archbishop of Lima, may be said to have been the founder of all the future glory of the Church in Peru. Her university owes its inception to him. Among the saints of Lima we may especially notice the half-caste, Martin de Porres, who was a Dominican lay-brother. The elevation to the altar of this coloured man is a powerful condemnation of those prejudices which have disgraced the Christian world for centuries.

More noteworthy perhaps than any is St. Louis Bertrand, the Dominican who laboured in South America in the middle of the sixteenth century. Of him it is recorded that the natives converted through his direct instrumentality were too numerous to be counted. One reason for this success was that he possessed the gift of tongues, and so was able to dispense with an interpreter.

XV

THE CONQUISTADORS

THAT Columbus' motives were, in the main, religious motives appears, not only from the character of the man and the circumstances relating to the organization of the expedition, but also from the letter he wrote announcing his find to the Spanish court. He begins by stressing the material advantages likely to result from his conquest, from which it appears that he has no qualms of conscience concerning the enterprise itself. He promises the king as much gold as he wants, as well as spices, cotton and mastic, and as many men for the navy as His Majesty may require. Then he goes on:

"Therefore, let the king and queen, our princes, and their happy kingdoms, and all the other provinces of Christendom, render thanks to our Lord and Saviour Jesus Christ, who has granted us so great a victory and such prosperity. Let processions be made and sacred feasts be held, and the churches be adorned with festive boughs. Let Christ rejoice on earth, as He rejoices in heaven, in the prospect of the salvation of the souls of so many nations hitherto lost. Let us all rejoice, as well on account of the exaltation of our faith as on account of the increase of our temporal prosperity, of which not only Spain but all Christendom will be partakers."

All the same, terrible discouragements dogged the steps of the missionaries from the start. The wrongs inflicted on the helpless dispossessed natives filled them with a loathing for the religion of their oppressors which it took years to overcome. The extent and grievousness of these wrongs are set out in detail in most Church History manuals. If they are touched on here, it is only because some knowledge of them is essential to an understanding of the heart-breaking problems confronting the apostolic men who laboured and died in these immense new missionary fields.

Impartial authors are unanimous in exonerating the missionaries themselves; and almost so in exonerating the King and Queen of Spain. If it had not been for the protests made and the active restraints exercised by the former, the native population might have dwindled to vanishing point, after the manner of the Redskins of North America; and the truth about the Spanish court is that, although it was all-powerful in Spain, there was not a great deal that it was able to do in the new dominions. There, the aborigines were at the mercy of the rabble of adventurers and place-hunters who took even the natural law into their own hands. Columbus had to man his ships as best he could, and in the first voyages the crews and passengers were sorry specimens for the most part. Those who followed were not much better, so that a sort of tradition of rascality was established which it was not easy to break later on.

The missionaries were hardly on the spot before they began to protest. They kept protesting all the time, and their protests were of the most outspoken character. However wrong-headed Spain was, or was tending to become, at that date, it redounds to the credit of the court that its monarchs— the proudest in Christendom—listened to these protests and went on allowing them to be penned. In one of his *Relations* addressed to the king, Las Casas compares the colonists to savage wolves, lions and tigers enraged by hunger. Then he goes on:

"They applied themselves, for forty years together, to massacring the poor wretches that inhabited the islands, putting them to all kinds of unheard-of torments and punishments; insomuch that this island (Hispaniola) which before the arrival of the Europeans contained three millions of people, is now reduced to less than three hundred. The island of Cuba, the length of which is equal to the distance between Valladolid and Rome, is entirely desert and destitute of its inhabitants, and nothing but ruins now to be seen on it. The islands of St. John and Jamaica have met with like treatment, and were very fertile and populous, but are rendered desolate and waste by the like means. Above thirty islands near that of St. John are entirely depopulated, though of a vast extent, so that there is scarce an inhabitant to be found in them. As for the continent, it is certain and what I myself know to be true, that the Spaniards have ruined ten kingdoms there bigger than all Spain, by the commission of all sorts of barbarity and unheard-of cruelties.

"They have driven away or killed all the inhabitants, so

that all these kingdoms are desolate to this day, and reduced to a most deplorable condition. As for Your Majesty, the natives, when they see the cruelty and impiety of your subjects, think you are the most impious Prince on earth and that you live upon nothing but human flesh and blood."

He has a lot more to say, all in much the same strain. He instances the case of a native chief refusing to be baptized on the eve of his execution, on the grounds that the heaven to which, he was told, the sacrament entitled him could not be anything but an undesirable place as long as there were Spaniards in it.

There were those, no doubt, who thought that if anything were to be done at all, it could only be by means of swords and soldiers. Later on in this book, we shall find a missionary of experience doubting the possibility of converting China in any other way. But when the Jesuits arrived in Brazil, they pushed on into the heart of the country without waiting for armed protection. And they did wonders, although they had no spectacular mass-conversions to report. Fathers Nobrega and Anchieta ventured alone and unguarded into the midst of one of the fiercest of the tribes. Fr. Anchieta so won them over by his gentleness and sanctity that he was never molested. He laboured for forty years in North and South America, and when he died a hundred thousand converted Indians mourned his loss. It is admitted, in fact, that had it not been for such men, the Portuguese could never have held Brazil, but must have been driven into the sea by sheer weight of numbers.

Early on the Jesuits saw the futility of trying to make real converts out of those who were being treated so barbarously; or, as they reported to the king, "were being exploited to the limit of extinction." Before consenting to go to Mexico, they obtained a royal decree according to which all converts were to be legally enfranchised from their imposed slavery. What they did in Paraguay is known to the whole world. Their *Reductions* were planned in an effort to protect the natives from their rascally exploiters. When they pointed out to the civil authorities that slavery must cease if the natives were to be pacified and converted, indignant protests filled the air, some of them emanating from the resident clergy who had got it into their Spanish heads that, to have their liberty taken from them, was about the best thing that could happen to such savages. A royal ordinance had provided that no converted Indian could be enslaved, and so the Jesuits determined to found reservations or enclosures, and then get the Indians to move into them, lead their own life and receive instruction. This was the origin of the *Reductions*, so called because the natives were recalled (*reducir*) from the jungle, into which their oppressors had driven them, to live in proper communities under Christian laws. At this very time, well-organized bodies of Spanish slave-hunters were at work in these territories, and in 1630 they murdered or carried into slavery thirty thousand natives. Such doings naturally caused the Indians to flock to the *Reductions*, which extended as far as Bolivia on one side, and northern Patagonia on the other, and from the Atlantic to the Andes.

The sequel is well known. In the middle of the eighteenth century a political war was declared on the Jesuits culminating in their suppression. The *Reductions* declined and eventually disappeared, leaving only ruins and memories behind them.

Another gallant attempt to mitigate the criminal wrong-doing incidental to the conquest was made by another Jesuit, this time in the extreme north of South America. Peter Claver was born on a farm in Catalonia in 1581. After an education in the University of Barcelona, he joined the Jesuits and, in 1610, landed at Cartagena a town in what is now known as the Republic of Colombia. In due course he was ordained priest.

At this period, what Pope Pius IX stigmatized as "the supreme villainy" had been in existence for nearly a century. The slave-trade, which the Church had taken hundreds of years to stamp out, was revived in its most revolting form by two of the foremost nations of Europe, Portugal and Spain. The port of Cartagena, owing to its favourable situation, was one of its great clearing-houses. Negroes from Angola and the Congo were bought in West Africa for four crowns a head and then shipped across the ocean to Cartagena. The conditions on board the vessels were such that fifty per cent of the human cargo perished on the way.

Still, an average of ten thousand Africans reached Cartagena every year, the majority of whom were at once transferred to the gold and silver mines. It is alleged that, during two centuries, the Spanish government concluded more than ten treaties authorizing the sale of some 500,000 of these negroes and received for the transactions a tax of over fifty million livres. It was not long before England joined in. The first of her ships sailing on this errand was called the *Jesus* and was in charge of Sir John Hawkins. Queen Elizabeth I knighted him for his exploits, and his crest exhibited the image of a manacled slave. From the beginning of the sixteenth century to the beginning of the nineteenth, between five and six million negroes, so it is calculated, were carried from Africa by different European powers and sold as slaves in the Americas. In the opinion of an American writer, ''so gigantic a crime, committed in the full light of modern Christianity, is one of the most discouraging facts in history.''

As for Peter Claver, as soon as he saw what was going on he declared himself "the slave of the negroes for ever." When the cargoes arrived, the blacks were shut up in the sheds lying along the quays, many ill, many dying. They were so crowded together that they had to sleep one on top of the other. The conditions were so revolting that one experienced Jesuit, who had been working in the sheds for forty years, "was covered with a cold perspiration and a death-like pallor every time a slave-trader was seen approaching the harbour." Into these sheds Peter Claver plunged with food and medicines, bread, brandy, lemons and tobacco. Many of the victims were too far gone to be able to accept them; these he baptized and anointed. The owners, for the most part, were adamant and would allow nothing to be done for their captives beyond the administration of baptism. The result was that this sacrament became for the poor wretches "a very sign and symbol of their oppression", as Father Thurston says. It is estimated that Peter instructed and baptized 300,000 of them. Pope Leo XIII made him the patron of all missionary work among negroes throughout the world.

An interesting sidelight on the atrocities, and on the lingering memories they have left behind, is provided by a news-item appearing in the Vatican newspaper *Osservatore Romano* in 1949, and reported in the *Universe* in October of the same year. "There is living today", quotes the latter journal, "a community of conscientious and faithful Catholics which has as little to do with priests as it can. These people are the Paez Indians of Colombia, in South America. They are a warlike tribe, whose stubborn bravery even caused the Spanish *conquistadores* to give up their efforts to subdue them. The Paez Indians, as good Catholics, hold the priesthood in the highest esteem. But they will allow no missionary to live among them. Their antipathy is to the white men in general and it took root in the past when they suffered many evils at the hands of intruders. Even today bandits and men escaping from justice enter the Indians' territory and there commit all kinds of outrages. Would-be immigrants have tried to seize their lands. Other whites have behaved with such disregard for morality that the Paez Indians' prejudice against aliens is now almost invincible. But they welcome visiting missionaries, who baptize their children and adminster the sacraments to the whole community. They prepare especially for the missionaries' visits on feast days, which they celebrate with great fervour. But they make it a condition that no attempt be made to establish a residential mission in their territory. To one missionary who asked whether they would accept him as their pastor, they replied: 'When we need you, we will call you'. The Paez Indians live in the prefecture of Tierradentro."

XVI

THE COMING OF THE JESUITS

MOST college boys are familiar with the passage in Macaulay's Essays wherein that stylist describes the missionary zeal that animated the members of the Society of Jesus almost from the moment of its inauguration.

"Dominant in the south of Europe, the great Order soon went forth conquering and to conquer. In spite of oceans and deserts, of hunger and pestilence, Jesuits were to be found in every country. The Old World was not wide enough for this activity. They invaded all the countries which the great maritime discoveries of the preceding age had laid open to European enterprise. They were to be found in the depths of the Peruvian mines, at the marts of the African slave-caravans, on the shores of the Spice Islands, in the observatories of China. They made converts in regions which neither avarice nor curiosity had tempted any of their countrymen to enter; and preached and disputed in tongues of which no other native of the West understood a word."

The leader of the Order never regarded the evangelization of the distant territories, now become accessible to the apostolate, as a mere side-line, as a sphere of activity to which third-raters, who were proving useless at home, might be prudently relegated. In one of his letters, Francis Xavier cautioned a superior against that particular snare. In general, Jesuit missions were distinguished by the lavish expenditure of men of the highest class devoted to their foundation and upkeep. As we shall see, the approach which the Society made to the Far East was, above all, a cultural and scientific one.

Then again, just as the stories sailors used to tell made boys want to run away to sea, so the scholarly accounts which the Jesuits began to send home from their missions were calculated to excite the interest of high-minded and heroic souls, and attract them to the missions. About the middle of the sixteenth century, some letters written by Xavier reached Rome and were circulated about the city. St. Philip Neri was one of those who read them, or heard them being read; and he was so moved that, in spite of his age, he was on the point of following Xavier's example. He was only prevented by a decision, more or less supernatural, to the effect that his India was to be Rome.

In the beginning of the sixteenth century, Portugal—thanks to Vasco da Gama—had established a chain of commercial depots stretching from Mozambique to Malacca, while her flag was to be seen all along the Indian coast from Goa to Ceylon. In the middle of the same century, the Russians, under Ivan the Terrible, the first Czar, crossed the Urals and occupied West Siberia. Later, they advanced as far as Lake Baikal, the Amur and the Pacific. Altogether, it looked as though the prospects of Asia's conversion were very promising indeed.

The Franciscans, who were the pioneers of missionary work in the East Indies, accompanied the Portuguese when they took possession of Goa. One of them became the first bishop of that see. At this time, a college for the education of priests was founded on the Molucca Islands and this became the model of another erected later at Goa. The old Thomas or Malabar Christians were very numerous in these parts, amounting it is said to 22,000 souls with 127 churches. They were nominally Nestorians under the jurisdiction of the Patriarch of Babylon and used the Syriac language. One of the Franciscans immediately got in touch with these communities, and made numerous conversions. Such was the position when Francis arrived in 1542. Orthodox Christianity in the whole of the Indies, as they were called—India proper, China, Tartary, Tibet, Japan and all the adjacent islands—was represented by four priests resident in Goa, who were mainly occupied in preserving the elementary decencies among the depraved Portuguese colonists.

The first Franciscan missionary was St. Francis himself, as we have seen. The first Jesuit missionary was also a Francis and a saint, and incidentally the greatest missionary after St. Paul; at least, so it is claimed. A Spaniard in the best traditions of Spain, he was thirty-five years of age when he set sail from Lisbon on April 7th, 1541. He was quartered in the vessel, one of a fleet of five, which carried the newly-appointed Viceroy of the Indies who was going to take possession of his government.

In all, crew and passengers amounted to a thousand persons crowded into one ship. The alternatives of heat and cold, the stench of the putrefying water and flesh meat brought on fever and scurvy. After rounding the Cape, they landed and wintered on Mozambique. Putting to sea again, they reached the island of Socotra and made contact with the emblems and practices of the Christian faith. Thirteen months after leaving Portugal, they anchored at Goa which now became the headquarters of Jesuit undertakings in the Far East and beyond. From this base, members of the Society dispersed in all directions; Francis himself to the Pearl Coast, to Malabar, Ceylon, Malacca, the Moluccas, Malaya and Japan; and divers brethren of his to the court of Akbar the Great Mogul, to the Brahmins, to China, to the east coast of Africa, to Abyssinia, to the Zambesi, to Angola, to Tibet and to Ispahan in Persia.

By Pope Pius X Francis was proclaimed patron of foreign missionary work everywhere. In many respects a pioneer, he yet succeeded in reaping phenomenal harvests and these among peoples who were not swayed by material or political considerations. In Travancore, during one month, he baptized ten thousand natives with his own hand. He had this advantage, too, that miraculous powers were conferred upon him, including the gift of tongues, and these profoundly moved the susceptible Indians. The first thing he did on reaching Japan, in 1549, was to learn the language. Before long he had mastered it sufficiently to be able to translate the Apostles' Creed and to start preaching. Essentially a practical man, he laid out a considerable sum in the purchase of a rich suit of clothes without which, he found, the notables would have nothing to do with him. When he left, after a stay of two years and four months, he sent three Jesuits to take his place.

Altogether his apostolate lasted for ten years, and it was continually thwarted by the political intrigues and rivalries of the times and, above all, by those seemingly permanent pests of the foreign mission field—the loose-living, unscrupulous, commercial men who trade in order to exploit, and exploit in order to trade. One of his fellow workers thanks God that no Europeans entered Japan along with Francis; for, if they had done, these pagans must have wondered how Christians could pretend to look forward to heaven, since they lived now as if there were no values other than those of this world. In a letter written in 1545, Francis speaks plainly to John III, King of Portugal, of the malpractices of his representatives in that part of the world which, he says, cause people to say that "Your Highness does not use your imperial power in India in order to extend Christ's kingdom, but rather for the purpose of making money and securing temporal advantages."

His method of instruction is revealed in a letter written to the catechists of the Society in India. From this it appears that the candidates for baptism were first taken through the Apostles' Creed, article by article, until the whole was fully understood. The scope of the instructions was then widened to embrace the sacraments, commandments, and so on; but each subsequent lecture was always preceded by a resumé of the Creed. Besides his own example, Francis bequeathed to missionaries everywhere the following prayer he composed for the conversion of the heathen:

"O Eternal God, Creator of all things! remember that the souls of unbelievers were made by Thee and fashioned to Thy own image and likeness. Remember that Thy beloved Son Jesus hath suffered a most cruel death for their salvation. Suffer not Thy Son to be any longer despised by unbelievers, but graciously hear the prayers of holy men and of all the Church. Remember Thy mercies and Thy compassion, and remember no more their idolatry, their unbelief, their hardness of heart. Give them grace at length to know, to fear and to love Him whom Thou hast sent; Jesus Christ Thy Son, our Lord, who is our salvation, our life and resurrection, through whom we are saved and made free, to whom be all glory for evermore."

In a memorandum on Japan addressed to St. Ignatius, he stressed the point that only really learned men should be sent to evangelize that country. "They should be well versed in philosophy, especially in dialectics. I should like them also to know some astronomy; for the Japanese are wonderfully desirous of knowing all about the causes of eclipses of the sun and moon, why the moon so often grows larger and smaller; or again, whence come the rain, the snow, the hail; what comets are, and what are the causes of thunder, lightning and the like. It is incredible how far the explanation of such things goes towards conciliating their good will."

When Francis returned to India in the year 1551, he found that the Church there numbered over half a million Christians, and had already produced a martyr in the person of Father Criminale—the first of a long line of Jesuits to die for the faith. Meanwhile, the evangelization of Japan went on apace. A college and university were opened; and, when one of the Daimios or "Great Names" was baptized, the conversion of the Empire began to look like a possibility. From the Southern Island a Japanese embassy was sent to Rome carrying a petition to the Pope for the canonization of Francis. Their journey took over three years, and they were given a tremendous reception in the Eternal City. Within forty years of his decease Japan contained four hundred thousand converts.

Disaster came with the close of the century when Taicosama, the Shogun, was threatening to invade the Philippine Islands. In the hope of averting this threat, the King of Spain sent some Franciscans to Japan to negotiate a peace. They laboured for three years and made many conversions. But the advisers of the Shogun persuaded him that these priests were really political agents, and he acted accordingly. It is calculated that, at this crisis, over three thousand suffered death for the faith, amongst them those known as the Japanese Martyrs. Three hundred thousand native Christians were reduced to poverty. This catastrophe annihilated the flourishing communities of Japan.

XVII

SOME JESUIT UNDERTAKINGS

ON reading the letters of Francis Xavier, St. Philip—as we have noticed—was on the point of embarking for the Far East as a missionary. One man who did so, and for the same reason, was Thomas Stevens, the first Englishman of any consequence to set foot on Indian soil. A Dorset man and educated at Winchester, he entered the Order and studied at the Roman College along with his countrymen Henry Garnet and Robert Persons. From Goa he wrote an account of his voyage to his father, a London merchant, which was printed both by Hakluyt and Purchas. This same letter largely influenced the London merchants in their decision to fit out an expedition designed to explore the possibilities of trade with India. For forty years Father Stevens worked among the Hindus, being the first of his countrymen to make a contribution to the literature of that people. He composed, in Sanskrit, an epic poem, in eleven thousand couplets, dealing with the subject matter of the Bible.

Fr. Stevens set out for Goa in 1579. In that very same year, two other Jesuits left Goa in order to try their hands at converting the Great Mogul. This mission failed, but later a nephew of Francis Xavier attempted the same task and nearly succeeded. At the request of the monarch, he translated the four Gospels into Persian, and wrote a Life of Christ in the same tongue which the Emperor read with great interest. After Akbar's death, three royal princes were baptized, riding to the church on white elephants. Eventually a college was founded at Agra, where Akbar died, and a mission station at Patna. At Lahore and Agra, two of the Mogul capitals, the Jesuits erected one of their famous Cribs, modelled on that at Goa, which made a great impression on the Hindus. Besides the usual figures, they contained artificial birds that sang, images of apes spouting water and figures of the Three Kings which shed real tears. At Christmas, 1610, the one at Agra was open to the public for forty days and was visited by hundreds of thousands.

In this period, the Jesuits began a series of persistent efforts to do something for Abyssinia, the eastern or upper Ethiopia of the ancients. In the fourth century, as we have seen, St. Frumentius won over its capital and its empire to the Christian faith. For hundreds of years the Ethiopian Church resisted all attempts made to corrupt it either with heresy or Islamism, but in the Middle Ages it was largely controlled by the Monophysites. And now at length, Jesuit missionaries turned their attention to this territory with a view to restoring the nation to the fullness of Christian unity and truth.

It is said that Vasco da Gama's memorable voyage of 1497 was undertaken with the object of discovering Prester John, but that he discovered the sea-route to India instead. This fabulous personage was, for long, supposed to be ruling over a Christian empire somewhere in the East; but, at the end of the fifteenth century, report had it that the Negus of Abyssinia and he were one and the same man. Vasco da Gama's search came to nothing, but the Portuguese Viceroy of India sent an expedition from Goa, with two Jesuits included in it, which sailed up the east coast of Africa, through the Gulf of Aden into the Red Sea, and anchored at the Eritrean port of Massawah. The missionaries then began a trek overland which took them through Aduwa to the banks of Lake Tsana, the source of the Blue Nile. At last they reached the court of the Negus and gazed with awe upon Prester John reclining in barbaric splendour amid a profusion of tiger-skins and silk tapestries from the looms of Ormuz and Cairo. The Fathers presented their credentials—a letter signed by the Pope and the King of Portugal—and requested leave to have free access to Ethiopia. They were sent back without a word being spoken as to the reasons for the refusal.

But the project was not dropped for all that. Another Jesuit mission succeeded in converting the Emperor Socinios, and in 1624 Abyssinia was reunited to Rome, only to fall away again. The country then remained closed to the missionaries until 1702. We have not mentioned the names of these various evangelists but one of their number was a Father Lobo, born in 1593, who wrote an account of his mission. In 1735, Doctor Johnson did an abridged translation of this work, and so made his *début* on the literary stage. Lobo's book was also the inspiration of Johnson's *Rasselas*.

Four years later, two Portuguese Jesuits and a lay-brother set out from Goa to convert the ruler and subjects of another African Empire, which stretched from north of the Zambesi to south of the Limpopo, from the east coast to the Kalahari desert. He was a Karanga monarch known to his people as the Monomotapa and to the Portuguese as the Gold King. The missionaries began work in the neighbourhood of Inhambrance and, in the beginning, met with a fair amount of success. Pushing on to the capital, one of the Jesuits succeeded in converting the Gold King and all his entourage. But the Mohammedan traders, who looked upon the Portuguese as their enemies, suggested to the king that the missionaries were really spies of that government sent out to prepare the way for an invasion. By his orders the Father was strangled and his body thrown into the river. Thus ended the first mission to that territory part of which Livingstone explored and where the Jesuits have a flourishing mission at the present day.

Next in order comes Father de Nobili and his bold move to convert the Brahmins, inspired by the Scripture precept: "all things to all men, to gain all to Christ." He entered the mission field of Southern India in 1606, and within twelve months had mastered the Tamil language and had acquired a sound working knowledge of Sanskrit. The Brahmins of this locality had, so far, been practically beyond the reach of the Christian apostolate; because they looked upon Europeans, meaning the Portuguese, as no better than unclean animals with whom no self-respecting Hindu could associate. These "foreign-devils" violated some of the most sacred practices and traditions of India, by eating flesh-meat and drinking alcoholic liquors. Worst of all they were seen to mix freely with the lower orders, such as the Pariahs, whom the Brahmins shunned as we would shun vermin. Besides, the conversion of a Brahmin inevitably meant a loss of caste, at least under the existing conditions.

De Nobili resolved to put in practice a new procedure that would remedy all this. He recognized the castes as social institutions, and he tolerated certain customs and practices to which, he considered, no real religious significance was attached. Assuming the garb of the Hindu ascetic and adopting their way of living, he moved into the Brahmin quarter, giving out that he was a Roman rajah who desired to practise penance, and study the sacred law. He called himself a Brahmin, and looked and spoke like one. He made a deep impression by the perfection and ease with which he spoke Tamil, by his familiarity with the best Indian authors and by his skill in reciting and singing fragments of native poetry. He was the first European to read and study the Hindu literature in the Sanskrit originals. He found in the Vedas many truths which he quoted in testimony of the faith he preached. He was the author of a number of religious works in the native languages, some of which are still in use. By the end of the seventeenth century, the mission he founded had made one hundred and fifty thousand conversions.

The concessions which de Nobili made to Hindu susceptibilities resulted in a controversy which had its low-minded as well as its high-minded side. The wrangle ended in the condemnation of the concessions by the Holy See. This brilliant man worked in Madura, Mysore, and the Karnatic until blindness compelled him to retire. From then on conversions among the higher castes diminished almost to vanishing point, until the Jesuits opened in 1838, at Negapatam, a college (now at Trichinopoly) for the education of the sons of Brahmins.

If, as is usually stated, the Dominican friar St. Hyacinth did succeed in entering Tibet, then he was the first European to do so. Failing him, the credit goes to the Franciscan Odoric of Friuli who is said to have reached Lhasa in the first half of the fourteenth century. It was at this period that the celebrated Buddhist reformer, Tsong-Kaba, appeared; and Tibetan legends affirm that he came under the influence of Christian teaching. A lama from the west, say these traditions, came into the land of Ambo (eastern Tibet) and dwelt in the tent of Tsong-Kaba's father. Influenced by his sanctity, Tsong-Kaba begged for instruction. The supposition is that, having been imperfectly instructed, Tsong-Kaba later introduced a new form of Buddhism containing Christian ingredients.

But it is not until two hundred years later that any certain information is forthcoming on the subject of this mysterious land, in a letter written by the Portuguese Jesuit Father Anthony d'Andrada who describes the journey he made into it. He begins by saying that, for twenty years, the Jesuits had been insisting that there were Christians in Tibet and that he resolved to find out for himself. Merchants, in fact, had been coming back to India and reporting that they had come across beliefs and customs that were unmistakably Christian, the beliefs and customs introduced, presumably, by Tsong-Kaba. In 1624, d'Andrada set out from Agra, crossed the lesser peaks of the Himalayas and reached the Tibetan capital to find the court and people well disposed towards him. He was given liberty to preach and a piece of ground for a church.

Several subsequent attempts were made to evangelize Tibet, but after the Capuchins were expelled in 1760, there was no contact with the country until the celebrated journey of the Lazarists Huc and Gabet in 1844.

It was the French Jesuit, Father de Rhodes, who was the pioneer of Christianity in Indo-China. He was sent from Goa in 1627. In less than twelve months he was able to converse in the Annamite language, the pronounciation of which, according to the scholars, resembles the chirping of birds. He addressed himself, in the first instance, to the educated and influential classes, and actually succeeded in converting two hundred Buddhist priests, many of whom joined him as catechists. With an eye to the future, he opened a college for the training of catechists. These were exercised in the theory and practice of medicine, so that they might the more readily have access to the homes of the people. This system worked so well that, in a short time, it produced three hundred thousand conversions.

While they never disdained the humbler tasks such as that of evangelizing the Indian Pariahs and the aborigines of South America, the Jesuits in the Far East made immediate contact with and sustained efforts to convert the educated classes. In China and Japan, as much almost as in India, the conviction prevailed that the Europeans were an inferior race. In many cases, the orientals had only the worst specimens to go by in the shape of the degenerate Portuguese colonials, and their everyday vocabulary was full of opprobrious epithets which were applied to westerns indiscriminately. They did not believe that Europe could teach them anything worth learning. The thing was to make them see their mistake, and this the Jesuits determined to do. They selected China for a try-out of their experiment which has been described as a semi-desperate enterprise.

For indeed, at this period, the conversion of that vast empire was beginning to be despaired of even by the most zealous and most optimistic. Attempt after attempt had failed; Franciscans, Dominicans, Augustinians and even Jesuits had tried their hands at the task with results equally unfortunate for all. A wonder-worker like Francis Xavier might have repeated there the success he achieved in Japan; but, when he was in sight of the goal of his main ambition, his eyes closed in death. In 1575, a Jesuit missionary, who had been compelled to abandon the Chinese mission, wrote to the General of the Society a letter in which he delivered himself of a very revealing statement. After enumerating all the fruitless efforts that had so far been made, he concluded with these words: "One can see no hope of converting them save by force of arms, and unless they yield to the force of these arms"—to such a degree had the idea of conversion come to be associated with the idea of conquest. But the Jesuits never really cared for the conquistador business, and they resolved to approach China once more, backed up by the machinery, not of war, but of peace. They were all the more determined, inasmuch as they appreciated the fact that China was, at that time, arbiter of the fate and destinies of missionary enterprise in Western Asia.

Into China, therefore, the Jesuits went, not indeed as the pioneers but certainly as the real founders of the Christian mission in that country. Had things gone smoothly, they might have converted the whole population. Such, however, was not the will of God. As it was, they did memorable service, especially in the cultural field. They translated Aesop's *Fables* into Chinese, as well as the Missal and Breviary. They furnished forth the first good atlas of China that had appeared. They also translated into Latin the Confucian classics, which were thus made available to European scholars for the first time.

Although Father Matteo Ricci entered the Celestial Empire in 1582, he did not succeed in gaining a footing in the capital until 1601; and this he did solely on the merits of his scientific reputation. He procured the goodwill of the Emperor by the gift of a map of the world on which the latter saw, for the first time, the size, the shape and position of his own dominions and, what surprised him most, the existence and dimensions of so many other kingdoms besides. Mathematics and astronomy had, for centuries, engrossed the attention of the Chinese government; but Ricci was able to prove that, in these matters, the Europeans had many valuable lessons to impart. His map aroused hostility at first, but he was able to describe it as the most useful work that could have been done to dispose China to give credence to the things of the faith.

Father Adam Schall, a native of Cologne, joined the Chinese mission about the year 1619 and was summoned to Pekin, some ten years later, in order to supervise the reform of the Calendar. This he did in collaboration with an Italian Jesuit. The upshot was that he was made President of the Board of Mathematics, and received an official rank corresponding to that of a mandarin.

Father Schall was succeeded by a Belgian colleague named Verbiest who designed and constructed a whole series of instruments, a large-sized quadrant, compass, sextant and celestial globe. All these were made of brass and beautifully designed, and they are still preserved in Pekin.

Just when the prospects in China seemed at their brightest, the question which had agitated the minds of Christian missionaries, almost from the time of the Apostles, came to a head and produced a controversy lasting for over a hundred years. Father Ricci, the first superior of the Jesuits in that country, owed his astonishing success partly to the patient forbearance he exercised with regard to the social and official customs bound up with Confucianism and the practice of ancestral worship. It was amongst the educated and administrative classes (the mandarinate) that Ricci's influence was most felt; and he very soon realized that it would not be possible to convert these unless some concession were made to certain age-long ceremonial customs. When another Jesuit, Father Paul le Jeune, was trying to convert the Redskins of North America, one of their number said to him: "What am I but a big tree strongly rooted in the ground? Wield your axe on me and go on wielding it, and eventually you bring me down. Do you think you can do it with a single stroke? I want to fall but cannot. My roots keep me standing in spite of myself. But do not lose courage. One day you will win through."

Ricci, doubtless reasoning along such lines, took the view that, short of anything vital being at stake, the practical and prudent policy was one of toleration. After his death, different views began to prevail among the Chinese missionaries, especially the Franciscans; and the dispute was embittered by party rivalry and jealousy. In Europe a war of pamphlets on the subject began to be waged, and eventually the dispute was carried to the Holy See and settled by a number of declarations culminating in a Bull of Pope Benedict XIV issued in 1742, a document described as a "terrible blow to the missions to China." The Constitution of Pope Clement XI issued in 1715 obliged all missionaries to China to take an oath, the terms of which were a renunciation of such ceremonies as were held to be tainted with superstition and idolatry.

XVIII

FIRST MISSIONS IN NORTH AMERICA

IN 1513, Juan Ponce de León sailed from Porto Rico, which he had conquered, and discovered and took possession of what he believed to be an island. This happened at Eastertide, a festival the Spaniards call *Pascua Florida* or Flowery Easter; and so he christened his "island" Florida. It is said that this explorer had really been commissioned to discover and annex the island of Bimini, a mythical region in which—so the Europeans thought—was located the fountain of perpetual youth. Although there are indications, in certain maps, that this territory was known to Europeans before 1513, the landing of Ponce de León is the first certain instance of a Christian setting foot on the soil of what is now the United States.

This is not to suggest that the claim made by the Icelandic Sagas is to be dismissed without a word. According to these, the Northmen discovered Labrador, Nova Scotia and a country which they called Vinland. Missionaries went to Vinland from Greenland and a bishopric was erected in it in 1121. A study of the narrative has led some to conclude that, in order to reach this Vinland, they must have turned Cape Cod and entered the waters of Narragansett Bay. In corroboration of this, a ruin has been pointed out near Newport for which a Scandinavian origin has been claimed.

Ponce de León made two attempts to colonize Florida each of which failed. Successive explorations established the fact that the territory was not an island at all but a continent, the North American continent, in fact. It was the Spanish admiral Menéndez who settled the fate of Florida. In 1565 his fleet anchored in a harbour to which he gave the name of St. Augustine in honour of the saint of the day (August 28th). On September 8th, a procession was formed led by the chaplain, Father López de Mendoza, and when the first Mass celebrated in North America was over, the Spanish flag was unfurled and Florida became a Spanish possession, and continued to be such, off and on, for nearly three hundred and fifty years. The city that grew up on the site of the landing is the oldest in the United States, Santa Fe in New Mexico being the second oldest. The Franciscans now proceeded to gather the natives of Florida into settlements and to baptize them.

Four years later, Pope St. Pius V, the same who excommunicated Queen Elizabeth I, sent the following letter to the Viceroy: "We rejoice to hear that our beloved son in Christ, Philip (King of Spain) has appointed you Governor of Florida, for we hear such an account of your person that we believe that you will do all to effect the increase of our holy Catholic faith. I am well aware, as you know, that it is necessary to govern these Indians with good sense and discretion; and that those who are weak in the faith may be strengthened, and that the unbelievers may by example be brought to the knowledge of the truth. But nothing is more important in the conversion of these Indians than to endeavour, by all means, to prevent scandal being given by the vices and immoralities of such as go to these western parts. This is the key of this holy work, in this is included the whole essence of your charge. Given at Rome in the year of our Redemption 1569."

That these sentiments were shared by the supreme authority in Spain is evident from the letters patent granted by the King to his representative, Vásquez de Ayllon, authorizing him to explore and colonize the Florida coast. This document is dated 1532 and is as follows:

"Whereas our principal intent in discovering new lands is that the inhabitants and natives thereof may be brought to understand the truth of our Holy Catholic Faith and become Christians and be saved, this is the chief motive you are to have in this affair. To this end, it is proper that religious persons should accompany you, as well as vestments and other things necessary for the observance of divine worship. I command that whatever you shall spend in transporting and maintaining the said religious persons, shall be paid entirely from the rents and profits which shall belong to us in the said land."

For a long period, under the general name of Florida was included the whole south-eastern portion of the United States, extending westwards beyond the Mississippi; so that by the Florida Mission was meant all the missionary activities conducted in that area, the operational centre of which was St. Augustine's. As early as the year 1526, a Dominican priest named Anthony de Montesinos visited one of Ayllon's colonies in Virginia and no doubt celebrated Mass there. In the middle of the same century, a start was made in Georgia by the Franciscans, one of whom wrote some valuable works, which were the first books in any Indian dialect published in the United States. By the year 1655 there were thirty-five missions in Florida and Georgia, with 26,000 native Christians. They were wiped out by the English under Moore in 1704.

The Jesuits began work in South Carolina and Virginia about the middle of the sixteenth century, but these missions were short lived. Next, a small missionary expedition was undertaken into Virginia where its personnel was massacred within a year. Something was attempted in Texas as early as 1544, when a Franciscan from Mexico crossed the Rio Grande and converted many. But permanent missions were not established here until the close of the seventeenth century, when the natives were gathered together into reservations. They reached their peak fifty years later with a population of fifteen thousand converts. In New Mexico, also, the Franciscans were the first on the scene, arriving in 1542. In 1680 occurred the great Pueblo revolt when over four hundred Christians were massacred, including twenty-one missionaries. Arizona was not reached until 1732.

Long before this, two Spanish navigators had sailed up what was to be known as the Hudson River, and placed the countries lying on its shores under the protection of St. Anthony. It is just possible that the services of religion may have been performed on or near the site of New York at this time. But, as far as can be known, the first missionary to enter the territory of New York State was the Franciscan Joseph de la Roche, who made a daring exploration of this region then occupied by the Iroquois. This was in 1626. Sixteen years later, the Jesuit St. Isaac Jogues visited Manhattan Island and heard the confession of two Catholics whom he found there. He narrowly escaped death on this occasion, but he returned again in 1646, was martyred and his body thrown into the Mohawk river. The place where this happened is now the property of the Society of Jesus who serve the memorial chapel erected on the actual spot. Forty years after this tragedy, three English Jesuits moved in and started a school. In 1654, a chapel was opened on the banks of the lake where the city of Syracuse now stands. It was only after a long interval that anything in the least way permanent could be done in this territory. Eventually such Iroquois converts as there were had to withdraw to the vicinity of Canada.

The first attempt to spread the faith in what is now the State of Maryland dates from 1570, when some Jesuits arrived in Chesapeake Bay; but they landed only to suffer martyrdom. Subsequent attempts sponsored by Lord Baltimore were successful, until the Indian war of 1642 put an end to the apostolate for the time being. In 1612 two Jesuits entered the State of Maine and founded a mission which was responsible for the conversion of the Abnaki tribe.

The earliest Christian settlement in New England was made by the Jesuits in 1613. This was raided by the English a few months later and the missionaries carried off. The Franciscans then began to minister to the French fishermen living along the coast, and did some work among the Indians in New Brunswick and Nova Scotia. The Jesuit Gabriel Druillettes then established a missionary station on the Kennebec which held its own for eighty years. The chronic warfare going on between the French and English reduced work to a standstill here, and the bulk of the tribesmen retreated into Canada. In what used to be known as the North Western Territory, that is to say the region of the Ohio river and lake, the first mission was established in Upper Michigan by Father René Menard in 1660. Other Jesuits went into Wisconsin, Indiana, Minnesota and Illinois about the same time.

The pioneers in the Northern and Central Plains were the Franciscans who accompanied Coronado in his expedition, and remained behind to work in southern Kansas. This was in 1540. The Sioux or Dakota Indians, whose original territory extended from Wisconsin to the Rockies, were visited by the Jesuits in 1666.

Originally, the name California was applied to all the territory, claimed by the Spaniards, bordering on the Pacific Ocean and lying north of Cape San Lucas. Later it was used to designate the area now included in the State of California and the peninsula of Lower California. The latter had been evangelized by the Jesuits between 1697 and 1767. Upon their expulsion, the care and conversion of the Indians devolved upon the Franciscans, to whom belongs the honour of founding the great mission system of California proper. The leader of this undertaking was Fra Junipero Serra who established his first mission at San Diego in 1769. San Francisco was founded in 1776.

Serra was born on the island of Majorca and joined the Franciscans in 1730, "taking the name of that quaintest and drollest of all Francis' first companions of whom the saint said: 'Would that I had a whole forest of such Junipers.' " He was one of a large contingent of missionaries who embarked at Cadiz bound for Vera Cruz. The voyage lasted for ninety-nine days. On arrival, Serra worked in Mexico for twenty years and then took over the Californian Missions vacated by the Society of Jesus. Nine missionary centres were established by him before his death in 1784. They were founded in the following order: San Diego, San Carlos de Monterey, San Antonio de Padua, San Gabriel, San Luis Obispo, San Francisco, San Juan Capistrano, Santa Clara, San Buenaventura.

The record of this man's activities throws a great deal of light on missionary procedure in the New World generally, at all events on the procedure followed by the Franciscans. In his apostolic journeys, Serra was invariably accompanied by a small detachment of soldiers. On arrival in a district, a cross was erected, as well as a rough shelter for the celebration of Mass. The Indians were summoned by the ringing of a bell swinging from a tree. Their good will having been secured by means of simple presents, the mission station was formally founded and dedicated to some saint. Two friars were usually left in charge with a few soldiers to keep order. Before long, this rough beginning would give way to something more permanent; but half a century passed before the conversions justified the erection of those beautiful groups of buildings, the remains of which are to be found in California today. The suggestion that these Indians were compelled to become Christians is refuted by the figures of the actual conversions, which are most disappointingly low. Serra himself succeeded in baptizing only one thousand of them. He died at the San Carlos station in 1784.

One hundred years later, the legislature of California passed a resolution making August 29th of that year, the centenary of his death, a legal holiday. His work for the Indians earned him the title of "Godfather of American Civilization."

In general, the natives of California were law-abiding and well-conducted. The San Gabriel Indians, in particular, were quite a superior people, although they believed neither in hell nor the devil, regarding these as the perquisites of the white man. Marriage between kinsfolk was unheard of, murder was punished by death and thieving was unknown. They knew the North Star and the points of the compass. They were very fond of games and their singing contests lasted for days on end. They were extremely polite and had a code of good manners which none was permitted to violate; a child, for instance, fetching water was not allowed to taste it on the way, and it was considered bad form to pass between two people conversing together.

XIX

AMONG THE REDSKINS

THE honour of planting the Christian faith in Canada, and the north-eastern portion of what is now the United States, belongs to France and, in the main, to the Society of Jesus. There are grounds for believing that Basque, Breton and Norman sailors had raised the cross on the shores of the country before the visit of Cabot the Elder in 1497, certainly before that of Jacques Cartier of St. Malo. Still, the latter must be looked upon as the real discoverer and first explorer of this part of the continent. It is said that he had Mass celebrated at Gaspé Peninsula, in the Gulf of St. Lawrence, in 1534. He made three voyages to Canada. The first carried him to Newfoundland, Labrador and across the estuary of the St. Lawrence to the north bank. In his second, he ascended the St. Lawrence as far as Hochelaga, now Montreal, and passed the winter at Stadacona, now Quebec. In his third, he made an ineffectual effort to colonize the country. About this time, some Jesuits and secular priests were attached to the settlements made in Acadia and Nova Scotia; but nothing important was done until Champlain laid the foundations of Quebec in 1608.

If Cartier was the discoverer, Champlain was certainly the father of New France. Almost from childhood, he felt the call of the sea. "Navigation," he wrote, "has always seemed to me to be the first of callings, since by it we obtain a knowledge of different countries, regions and kingdoms. By it we attract and bring to our own land all kinds of riches." But the sentiments that follow show that what appealed to him most of all was the opportunities navigation offered for propagating the faith; sentiments which, we may be sure, were shared by the majority of those early adventurers. "By means of navigation, pagan idolatry is overthrown and Christianity proclaimed. This is the art which led me to explore the coasts of New France, where I have always desired to see the lily flourish, together with the Catholic, Apostolic and Roman religion."

As a youth, he served his apprenticeship on board his father's vessel and, at the age of twenty-one, was given command of a ship fitted out by Spain to oppose the attack made on Porto Rico by the English. It was during this cruise that he suggested the possibility of uniting the Atlantic and Pacific by a canal across the Isthmus of Panama. He first arrived in Canada in 1603, and during the next forty years he explored and founded, and founded and explored, to such purpose that his life is the true beginning of that country's eventful history.

In 1615, he called in the Franciscan Recollects who inaugurated, in the interior, those missions to the Redskins which were soon to become famous. One of these Franciscans, Father le Caron, compiled the first dictionary in the Huron language; a colleague of his, Brother Gabriel Sagard, was the first to publish a history of Canada; while a third, Father Viel, was thrown into the Ottawa river by an apostate Indian, at a spot still known as Sault-au-Récollet. Finding themselves too few in number to carry on the work, the Franciscans sent two of their Order to France to enlist the co-operation of other bodies. In response to this request, the Jesuits and the Sulpicians volunteered their services. The latter devoted themselves, in the main, to the needs of the French settlers; but one of their Order, as we shall see, distinguished himself to such a degree that he is known as the Apostle of the Iroquois.

The field of apostolic labour which was now about to be opened up, and in which the French Jesuits were to distinguish themselves, was probably the most difficult that missionaries have ever had to cope with. Where there are now a succession of cities and towns, there was then nothing but virgin forest and prairie. Of civilized life there was not a trace. The inhabitants wandered around for the greater part of the year and settled for the winter in their rude villages. The tribes were so numerous that there is scarcely a river or lake in Canada that does not bear the name of some community. They all acknowledged the existence of One Supreme Being and one only, but they neither worshipped nor offered prayers and sacrifices to this God. Polygamy was the rule and purity was non-existent. Unheard-of cruelties were practised on their captives, and a man's importance was shown by the number of scalps hanging at his girdle.

The greatest difficulty of all was the languages. The various Redskin "nations" were cut up into a multitude of clans each with a dialect of its own. These dialects, although spoken by tribes who lived side by side and belonged to the same "nation", were so widely variant, the one from the other, that only the most careful scientific analogy is able to reveal their common parentage. To illustrate this permanent problem of missionary work in uncivilized territories, we append a table showing the initial words of the Our Father in twelve Indian dialects. Shea, from whose book—*The History of the Catholic Missions among the Indian Tribes*—these specimens are taken, gives about thirty different complete Our Fathers.

Algonquin:	*Kemitanksena spomkik ayan Waiwaiselmoquatch . . .*
Choctaw :	*Piki vba ish binili ma chi hohcaifo hut . . .*
Huron:	*Onaistan de aronhiae istare sasen . . .*
Blackfoot:	*Kinana spoegsts tzittapigpi kitzinnekazen . . .*
Mohawk:	*Songwaniha ne Karonyage tighsideron . . .*
Assiniboin:	*Tuchiachttoobe machoiachta yaenshi baeninshi . . .*
Chippeway:	*Nossinan gijigong abiian Apegich . . .*
Flatheads:	*Kyle-e-ou itchitchemask askwest . . .*
Menomonee:	*Nhonninaw Kishiko epian Nhanshtchiaw . . .*
Flatbows:	*Katikoe naitle naite akiklinais . . .*
Senecas:	*Gwahnik gaoyah gehshoh shidyoh . . .*
Potowatomies:	*Nosinan wakwik ebiyin ape Kitchitwas . . .*

The first members of the Society arrived in Canada in 1625, returned home for political reasons and, then, settled down for good in 1635 in which year a college was opened in Quebec by Father le Jeune. It was he who, after studying the natives on the spot, formulated the new plan of campaign. For the immediate purposes of missionary work he saw that the Redskins fell into two large groups. First of all there were the Algonquins roaming about, under various names, in the region north of the St. Lawrence, in the basin of the Ottawa river and in the territory lying between its mouth and the prairies of the north-west. Then, south of Lake Ontario and in the Niagara peninsula, there were the Huron-Iroquois. Altogether they numbered 100,000 at the least. Of these two main groups, the latter was the most stable and settled ; and the Jesuits considered that, instead of chasing around after

the wanderers, the first thing to do was to Christianize those
who were settled, or could be induced to settle. A stable community of that sort might become a missionary centre, and
its social advantages might appeal to the nomads. Now the
Hurons alone were characterized by a certain stability, and
the Jesuits decided to concentrate all their attention on them.
Thus began the immortal Epic of Huronia.

This Epic has found its way into print to the extent of a
small library of volumes, and can be studied in all its fascinating details. From the start, Jesuit missionaries were
accustomed to send home careful accounts of the work they
were doing, and of the conditions under which they were
doing it; St. Francis Xavier, for instance, whose correspondence is a valuable source of information for all that con-
cerns the Far East. He obliged his subordinates to send in
these reports, so that he may be regarded as the originator of
the practice where the Society is concerned; for, indeed, both
the Dominicans and Franciscans supplied Europe with much
valuable information while working in the Americas.

The letters of the Jesuits were of three kinds; confidential
ones meant for the eyes of superiors and personal friends,
annual reports for the benefit of the Jesuit communities in
Europe, and accounts of general interest designed for circulation. These last are known as *Relations*, and the reports
sent from Canada as *Relations of New France*. There is an
edition of them in seventy-three volumes, edited by Thwaites.
They were not written merely to satisfy people's curiosity,
but to stimulate interest in the missions, and induce the
French to take a hand in a work which was being monopolized
by Portugal and Spain. At the same time, their historical
importance is of the highest, for to them we are indebted
for nearly everything that is known of Canada and New
York State during the first century and a half of their penetration by Europeans.

The French missions, as these documents show, were
organized on quite a different plan from those of the
Spaniards. When the latter first attempted to evangelize
Florida and New Mexico, they went in ones or twos, trusting
to providence; but they soon found it necessary to adopt
another system; and, so, we next get organized bodies

consisting of soldiers, catechists, and mechanics, as well as missionaries proper. On arrival, they proceeded to set up a reservation containing a church, friary, workshops, granaries and a hospital; and the Indians were gradually induced to live inside this reservation. This was the procedure followed in Texas and California. But the French missionaries acted differently. They relied on persuasion. The villages they established were not reservations, and the natives were not interfered with; the tribes remained tribes, and the Christian Indians were as free as the pagan ones.

One of their number, Father le Jeune, has described the sacrifices the Jesuits were prepared to make in order to establish a mission-station among these natives. Their arrival had to be timed so as to take place in winter, for only then could they rely on finding the Redskins at home. In this instance le Jeune seems to have been alone. Having been accepted as a boarder, so to say, he was accommodated in one of the wigwams, which was really a great sunken ring made by digging the snow, and covered over by a series of poles converging at the top, and connected by a lattice of sewn bark. The roof was so low that it was impossible to stand upright; and there were four other discomforts: cold, heat, smoke and dogs. A roasting fire was burning in the centre, and this drove you to the circumference where you were half-frozen by the proximity of the wall of snow outside. Father le Jeune says that the smoke nearly killed him, and that he was crying all the time, although there was neither grief nor sadness in his soul. He had to recite such portions of his Breviary as he knew by heart. The intense cold drove the dogs indoors where they lay on top of the human inmates.

The cooking was so bad, and so carelessly performed, that he had to refuse the food offered to him, and live for a time on sea-biscuits and smoked eel. There were bad days when all he had was the skin of these eels, which he had used for patching his gown. "I was so hard-pressed," he says, "that I ate the patches."

The languages more or less mastered, the missionary then began the work of instruction. How this was conducted is revealed in another *Relation* written, this time, by the future martyr Father Brébeuf. Normally, the tribesmen were called together by the ringing of a bell, or by an order sent round by the Chief. When all had assembled, a beginning was made by chanting a rhythmical version of the Our Father translated into the Huron tongue; the priests intoned the first two lines, the people the next two, and so on. The Indians, especially the children, thoroughly enjoyed this part of the service at any rate. Then came the talk which the Father gave vested in surplice and biretta. The children were then questioned and those who answered correctly were given a glass bead.

The Huron mission was broken up for a time, when the English captured Quebec; but France regained her colony and the Jesuits were able to return to their posts. The history of their labours during the next few years "is connected with the origin of every town celebrated in the annals of French America; not a cape was turned, not a river entered, but a Jesuit led the way." Among the tribes, with the exception of the Iroquois or Five Nations, Christianity made remarkable progress. All the Hurons were converted. To put the missions on a permanent footing, a training college—the first in North America—was opened at Quebec in 1635. An Ursuline convent for the education of Indian children followed, as well as a public hospital. Quebec became an episcopal see in 1674.

Unfortunately the rivalry between the various European powers led to the policy of setting the Indians one group against another. After a struggle lasting for a quarter of a century, the Iroquois nearly wiped out the Catholic Hurons. A number of the missionaries were martyred under circumstances as atrocious as anything recorded in the history of the apostolate. Fathers Brébeuf and Lalemant had red-hot hatchets applied to their armpits and loins, and necklaces of red-hot lance blades put round their necks. Brébeuf preached to his tormentors until they tore off his lips and nose and, in derision of baptism, poured boiling water over his head. While the priests were yet living, pieces of their flesh were cut off, cooked and eaten by the Redskins, who also drank the blood of their victims while it was still warm.

These two, together with six other Jesuits, were canonized in 1930 and are known as the Martyrs of North America. As it turned out, the truths which these men proclaimed were later embraced by their very executioners. Within fifty years, so great a number of the Iroquois were converted that they migrated and founded a settlement of their own. This was in what is now western New York. When the English moved in, the missionaries were expelled and the Iroquois settlement migrated to Canada. In the meantime, other Jesuits were working in the vast prairie lying between the St. Lawrence and Lake Superior, and were establishing stations in what are now the States of Michigan, Wisconsin and Illinois. South of Lake Ontario, too, they restored the Iroquois mission at a place which was the home of Catherine Tegakwitha, a native Indian girl now known as the Lily of Canada, who may well be canonized one day.

Father Claude Allouez, the Apostle of the West, founded on Magdalen Island the first mission in the whole of the north-west. One of his associates was Father Marquette who, having erected the first European settlement in Michigan, and re-discovered and explored the Mississippi, descending as far as Arkansas and Illinois, did for the Mississippi Valley what he had done for Michigan. All the country adjoining the mighty river along which he had paddled in a canoe, he named Louisiana after his sovereign Louis XIV.

All this might lead one to conclude that the French Jesuits had everything to themselves in this area. They certainly bore the burden of the day and the heats. But there were others besides Jesuits. And there were other Jesuits besides French ones. Four English members of the Society, led by Father Andrew White, arrived in the *Ark and Dove* in 1633. They concentrated on Maryland. Father White compiled a dictionary and a catechism in the Piscataway language, as well as a grammar—now lost—which was the first attempt of its kind made by an Englishman. In his Journal, he gives an account of the River Missions which became a regular feature of his apostolate.

Three great disasters practically overwhelmed these missions; the fall of Quebec, the suppression of the Jesuits and the French Revolution. The posts vacated by the Fathers of the Society of Jesus were filled by members of the secular clergy and Sulpicians. One of these latter was Father Picquet, already mentioned, the Apostle of the Iroquois. Arriving in Montreal in 1734, he soon learned the Algonquin and Iroquois tongues so well that he surpassed the ablest orators of these tribes. He established a centre at Oka, fortified it and erected a Calvary that still exists. Later, he erected another on the Presentation River, and out of it grew the town of Ogdensburg, New York. We next hear of him travelling round Lake Ontario converting large numbers of Iroquois. During the war with the English, he organized detachments of his Indians and even accompanied them into battle. The English, in fact, set a price upon the head of this man who, the French Governor said, "was worth several regiments."

The fate of the aborigines is well known. When the Europeans first arrived, the aborigines occupied the whole country and were very numerous. In proportion as the whites extended their dominion, the savages retired, leaving after them sad monuments of their misfortunes and decay. It is said that only one-sixteenth of the Indians of California survived the American invasion of that territory. In the first half of the nineteenth century, the government of the United States resolved to form, to the west of Arkansas and the Missouri, a district exclusively Indian. Into this the scattered tribes were herded, after yielding up their villages and the hunting grounds so dear to their hearts. In 1838, the number congregated in this glorified concentration camp amounted to 100,000. In 1911 the entire native population of Canada was officially reckoned to be 111,000, of whom about 55,000 were Catholics.

XX

THE PORTUGUESE MONOPOLY

THANKS to the enterprise of her seamen, Portugal was the first and, for a long time, the sole European power exercising political authority in the East Indies. The evils connected with her expansion do not detract from the eminent services she rendered to the cause of the Christian apostolate in the immense regions subject to her exploration. The network of Missions, extending for thousands of miles from Goa right round the Indian peninsula to Cochin-China, Korea and Japan, owed everything, humanly speaking, to Portugal. She employed the prestige of her embassies, the authority of her name, the force of her arms and the wealth of her exchequer to promote and extend missionary undertakings. Much the same thing may be said of Spain whose kings endowed nearly all the churches in the New World, defrayed the travelling expenses of the missionaries and supplied the requisites of church worship. The Bull of Alexander VI awarded all the tithes accruing in the conquered territories to the Spanish monarch, on condition that the Church was supported out of them.

But, as the Abbé Huc remarks, in all ages one unavoidably sees the sad truth verified that the Church must pay for the success and protection she owes to the secular arm. In this case the splendid benefactions of the court of Portugal were off-set by consequences that, again and again, proved the ruin of many a flourishing mission. All went well while the Portuguese were in favour; Christianity was then in favour too. But every petty quarrel with this or that trumpery Portuguese official meant a quarrel with the missionaries. A serious breach of the political truce meant persecution and expulsion. Since the missionaries were nearly all Portuguese, other powers jealous of Portugal and anxious to supplant her were in the habit of suggesting that the priests were merely spies, or agents, sent to soften up the populace in preparation for an invasion. And it must be allowed that, in the end, Portugal's own behaviour was extremely reprehensible. Her rulers claimed and exercised *Rights of Patronage* according to which no bishop could be appointed without their approval, no mission-ary could go to the Indies without their consent, or in any except a Portuguese vessel.

As an illustration of this embarrassing problem as it affected China, we may quote the observations of a Christian Chinaman of our own time, the Benedictine monk Dom Pierre-Celestin Lou Tseng-Tsiang. In his book, *Ways of Confucius and of Christ*, he writes as follows:

"I should like to pass very rapidly over that sad and arduous period which stretches from the quarrel of the Europeans over the Rites down to the contemporary renewal. I will sum up the whole of this epoch by saying that it was a time of misunderstandings and, in consequence, of mistrust. The fact that those spreading the Gospel were subjects of foreign powers made their task extremely delicate, and very little was needed for them to be regarded by public opinion as the advance guards of a foreign domination. And, alas, some regrettable events brought about most sad confusions in this matter. It happened thus that, by force of circumstances, the Church became, in the eyes of the Chinese, the scapegoat for most of the political injustices of which my country was the object and nearly the victim." And, then, to show how persistent this problem is apt to be, Portugal or no Portugal, he tells us how, in 1917, when he exercised considerable political influence in his own country, he proposed to the government of China that it should come to an understanding concerning missionary matters with the Holy See. "The Vatican," he says, "indicated its approval. But the absolute and systematic opposition of a great European power obliged us to abandon the project."

Nothing jeopardized the future of the missions in the East so seriously as the absence of a native clergy. Under all the circumstances of this monopoly, it is difficult to see how this want could have been supplied. Over and above, it is perhaps permissible to doubt if Portugal, or Spain for that matter, would have taken kindly to such a priesthood, at any rate at that date. Apart from the injuries which so many of the representatives of those two nations inflicted on the coloured races, these representatives appear to have viewed them through rather distorted and un-Christian eyes.

These were the considerations at work in stirring up in Europe a movement whose object was to withdraw the Eastern missions from the absolute control of Portugal, and to create in these countries bishoprics independent of her patronage. Petitions from France were sent to Rome covered with signatures, amongst them that of St. Vincent de Paul. The petitioners asked Innocent X to reserve to himself the right of appointing some bishops for Tonkin and Cochin-China by way of a start. Propaganda hesitated and ultimately filed the petition. But the agitation was not allowed to die down and, eventually, this movement of reform was carried to success by the courage and energy of a woman, the Duchesse d'Aiguillon. Her solicitations were so pressing that she procured from the Holy See the nomination of three French bishops for the missions in Upper Asia. But it was essential to maintain the supply of missionaries, and to this end there was founded in Paris the *Société des Missions Etrangères* (1658), a world-famed missionary organization which, from the outset, paid particular attention to the business of recruiting native priests and bishops.

Going back to the three French bishops nominated at the instance of the Duchesse d'Aiguillon, these having prepared themselves for their work, along with twenty priests, got ready to embark. But the Portuguese refused to give them passports, and neither the Dutch nor the English would accept them as passengers. It was in consequence of this obstacle that one of their number, Pallu, Bishop of Heliopolis, conceived the plan of a commercial company, modelled on those of England and Holland, for sailing between France and the Far East. The plan was carried out, so that this maritime line, which afterwards became so famous in China and India, owed its formation to the inspiration and advice of a missionary.

Meanwhile the Portuguese business was to continue to be a source of difficulty for a long time. When the power of that nation began to decline, the supply of its missionaries naturally fell off, and yet it was not easy for others to take their place. A conflict of jurisdictions developed, in the end, known as the Goan or Indo-Portuguese Schism. After a series of attempts to patch up the rent, the *Padroado*, as it was called, was brought to an end in 1950 when all her rights of ecclesiastical patronage in India were renounced by Portugal herself. In view of India's newly-acquired independence, this settlement was inevitable.

Whatever may have been the vexations which came to a head in this century, they were to find ample compensation in the creation of two organizations of the very first importance where Foreign Missions were concerned. In 1622, Gregory XV inaugurated the Congregation of Propaganda, the object of which was to guard, direct and foster missionary work everywhere. One of its primary objects was to promote the establishment of seminaries in which men, preferably natives, might be trained for the missions. In Rome itself, Urban VIII set up one such, known sometimes as the Urban College, sometimes as the College of Propaganda since its management was entrusted to that Congregation. While it is claimed, and rightly so, that the origins of these two measures can be traced back to the enlightened ideas of Raymond Lull, the thirteenth-century Franciscan, it was the Order of Discalced Carmelites which was most active in promoting the actual foundation of the Congregation, while the College owed a great deal to a member of the Theatine Order.

This central Seminary recruits its pupils literally "from every nation under heaven." The scholastic year 1948-49 began with one hundred and fifty-four students, and ended with one hundred and seventy-two, belonging to nearly forty different races. A publication issued in the same year gives the names of about eight hundred alumni scattered throughout the world, although the statistics for Russia, Rumania, Bulgaria, Yugoslavia, Albania and China are necessarily defective. The college possesses a library of over thirty thousand volumes, among which are translations of a great number of Chinese works and a large collection of oriental manuscripts. Attached to the library is a Museum exhibiting many missionary objects, including an extraordinary assortment of idols. Each year, at the feast of Epiphany, the College hold what is called a Polyglot Academy in order to stress the universal character of Christianity. The students make recitations in their mother tongues. Annually, too, each employee of the Congregation receives the gift of a fan, a custom apparently originating in the early days when the missionaries sent these articles home from China and Japan.

XXI

FRANCE MAKES HER DEBUT

THE French now began to take up foreign missionary work in real earnest, all the more so since the crisis indicated in the preceding chapter almost coincided with the building up of their colonial empire. Complicated though their work may have been, at times, through their preoccupation with the political prestige of their country, the Christian apostolate has never had a more self-sacrificing body of co-operators; or, for that matter, a more interesting—with respect, that is, to the nature of their undertakings, and to the peculiar qualities they put into them. What they did among the Redskins of North America, and their manner of doing it, has already been reviewed at some length. That record furnishes forth a fair picture of the general style of an apostolate always characterized by deep religious feelings, by a patriotism more cultural perhaps than political, by a certain animation or verve, and by a great "feel" for personal liberty.

Indo-China was identified by Josephus with the Ophir from which Solomon obtained his gold. It was visited in the sixth century by a monk of Alexandria, who was the first to supply Europeans with clear ideas of the position of this part of the Far East. The Franciscan Odoric of Friuli was here in the fourteenth century, and we are indebted to him for our earliest information concerning the habits of the people. Missionaries attempted something in the way of an apostolate in the sixteenth century, but their efforts were neutralized by the hatred infused into the natives by the cruelties of the Portuguese filibusters. Indo-China had to wait for the coming of the French. Two Jesuits arrived from France in 1618 and made such headway that, within the space of forty years, it was found necessary to establish two vicariates. Many native bonzes were converted, and these kept the faith alive during the persecution that soon followed. But the man who did most to establish the faith on a firm footing was Father Pigneaux who arrived in 1765. The period intervening between his coming and the edict of expulsion issued in 1820 was the Golden Age of Christianity in the Annamite empire.

To a Frenchman, the Franciscan Father Bonferre, belongs the distinction of being the pioneer in Siam, the Land of the White Elephant, which was destined to owe its proper evangelization entirely to his compatriots. Bonferre set out from Goa in 1550 and preached for three years in Peguan without any result. When Francis Xavier was lying ill at Sancian, his mind was full of Siam, but death came to him before he could do anything about it. At this time, some Dominicans laboured successfully here until their martyrdom. Persecution then put an end to the apostolate which was not resumed until the period now under review. In 1662 the country was made a Vicariate with a Frenchman in charge, and seven years later was assigned to the Paris *Société des Missions Etrangères*.

Practically nothing at all was done in Guiana until some French Dominicans arrived at Cayenne about the year 1635. Thirty years later, the Jesuits made their appearance, one of whom, Father de Creuilly, spent over thirty years cruising along the coast and landing at various points in order to preach and baptize. Things looked very promising here until the anti-Jesuit movement in Europe led to the expulsion of the missionaries.

Under the protection of their embassy, French missionaries entered Smyrna, spread themselves through the islands of the Greek Archipelago and established themselves in Syria. The revival of Catholic missions in Syria dates from the time of the Crusades and the erection of the Latin Patriarchate of Antioch. For practical purposes, this Patriarchate came to an end in the fourteenth century and was not revived until 1762, its first occupant being a French Lazarist, Father Bassu. His jurisdiction extended over all that country, as well as Cyprus, Egypt and Arabia. The French Capuchins, also, were particularly active in this area at this time; and, in the beginning of the nineteenth century, French Jesuits resumed the work that had been begun there by the Society at the end of the sixteenth. A Parisian lady of means endowed a bishopric at Babylon whose first incumbent was a French Carmelite.

St. Vincent de Paul has been mentioned as one of the signatories to the petition, addressed to Rome, urging the

erection in the mission fields of French bishoprics. Into
the expansion now going forward, he threw all his versatile
energy. The Lazarists—so called from the Priory of Saint
Lazare in Paris where St. Vincent lived—were his sons and,
early on, they began to devote themselves to the work of the
foreign missions. Vincent had never forgotten the captives
languishing in the dungeons of Tunis, Algiers and Biserta
whose lot he had once shared. As early as 1645, he sent them
one priest and one lay-brother. Other Lazarists followed, one
of whom was made Consul so that he might be able to work
unhindered.

But Madagascar appears to have been Vincent's first
foreign missionary concern. Some years after its discovery by
the Portuguese, a number of religious (Franciscans?) accompanied a colony of emigrants who settled in a part of the island.
These were all massacred. We next hear of another band of
missionaries setting sail from Europe in a vessel which was
attacked, off the coast of Portugal, by Algerian corsairs.
During the fight that followed, the powder magazine caught
fire and the ship blew up with the loss of all hands. In 1615,
the young son of the king was conveyed to Goa to be educated
by the Jesuits. On the strength of this service, that monarch
allowed two members of the Society to preach in his
dominions. But the court sorcerers so worked on the king's
mind that he forbade his subjects to have any dealings with
them. One died and the other made his escape back to Goa.
This field was now abandoned for the time being.

In 1642, the East India Company obtained from Cardinal
Richelieu a trading monopoly with Madagascar and the
neighbouring islands. One clause in the agreement required
the Company to maintain one or more priests in the colony,
to act as chaplains to the French settlers, and to preach the
Gospel to the infidels. In 1648, the Company, having asked
St. Vincent de Paul to provide the requisite missionary, he
wrote to one of his subjects, Father Charles Nacquart, en-
trusting him with a task which, he said, required the faith of
an Abraham, the charity of a St. Paul and the zeal, patience,
courtesy, poverty, solicitude, discretion, moral integrity and
self-sacrifice of a Francis Xavier.

Father Nacquart, with one companion, reached the island

after a six-months' voyage. Other Vincentians followed and, in 1657, a report sent to St. Vincent estimated the Catholic population of the island at thirty-five families, twelve negro and twenty-three French. After the death of St. Vincent, his successor continued to send out new missionaries, most of whom either succumbed to the climate or were put to death by the natives. The mission of Fort Dauphin, which had to be abandoned in 1674, was reopened in 1896 by the missionaries of the same Congregation.

When the Jesuits were suppressed, the Lazarists took over their missions in the Levant and in the Far East. They were summoned to Macao in 1784 and took charge of educational establishments there. They reached Pekin at the critical period of the controversy over the Chinese Rites. This last post was a difficult one to fill; since, if the Jesuit tradition were to be maintained, it was essential that the missionaries should be well versed in science.

An interesting postscript to this section is supplied by certain facts relating to a Father Robert Hanna who was the second Irish missionary to enter China. Born in Newry in 1762, he went to Paris and joined the Lazarists. Before long, he was nominated for the China mission. Father Hanna had studied astronomy at the *Collège de France* under the famous scientist Lalande. He sailed from St. Malo and, on arrival at Macao, was detained for five years, because the Portuguese authorities refused to issue the necessary passports. At last, through the intervention of the British envoy, he was allowed to embark, and he arrived in Pekin in the summer of 1794. The Superior of the Lazarists at Pekin was himself a capable astronomer, and had charge of the imperial Board of Science. For three years, the Irishman worked in the Observatory, but he contracted chest-trouble and died in 1797 at the age of thirty-five.

During St. Vincent's lifetime, a mission was despatched to the Western Isles of Scotland the Catholics of which had lost all contact with their religion. In 1651, Father Dermot Duggan, an Irishman, left Paris with two companions. They had disguised themselves as merchants and, on landing, they were given hospitality by the Laird of Glengarry. Later, the three separated, Father Duggan making for the Hebrides.

In a most interesting report to his Superior, St. Vincent, Father Duggan tells how he converted the Laird of Clanranald, Lord of the Isle of Uist, and McNeil, Lord of the Isle of Barra. In Eigg, Islay and Canna he "converted" about nine hundred people, of whom only about fifteen knew anything about the Catholic faith. He found men and women of a hundred and even one hundred and twenty years of age who had never been baptized. The inhabitants of Uist did not know how to make the sign of the Cross. At that time, he and his companions were the only priests in the whole of the Highlands and Islands, and he exhorts St. Vincent to send some more who can speak Gaelic, can endure hunger and thirst, and are willing to sleep on the bare ground. His dietary (one meal daily) consisted of barley-bread or oatcake with cheese or salted butter; and he wore the plaid as a protection against the weather. He had two helpers, one to ferry him from island to island and another to act as a catechist and Mass-server.

There is reason to believe that the knowledge of Christianity had found its way into Korea during the early part of the seventeenth century. Certain "wise men" in that country, having heard it talked about by travellers and merchants, had some Christian books conveyed secretly to them through the agency of the Korean ambassadors who, annually, presented themselves at the court of Pekin. When the eighteenth century was drawing to a close, one of these ambassadors embraced the faith while he was in Pekin, and, on returning home, began to spread the Good Tidings among a number of his associates. In time, he gathered about him a regular community of believers. A member of this community was then sent to Pekin to obtain further particulars. There he was carefully instructed and baptized by the French Lazarist, Father Chislain. Going back, this man, whose name was Ye or Ly, laid the foundation of the faith among his countrymen who, so far, were without the aid of either priest or missionary. At last Bishop Gouvea of Pekin sent them a priest in the person of a Chinese called Tcheou. This was in 1794. Four years were spent in studying the language, and three in instructing the community of believers and in making new converts.

10

The Chinese priest responsible for this had made his way into Korea disguised, and unknown to the authorities, who took the utmost precautions to prevent foreigners from entering their territory. He was betrayed by some of his own converts, and a search was immediately instituted with a view to his apprehension. In hopes of saving his life, one of his Christians shaved his head in the Chinese fashion, and more or less let it be believed that he was the intruder. But Father Tcheou was taken, tortured and put to death. Before he expired, he prophesied that, at the end of thirty years, the little Christian Church in Korea would receive assistance. His prediction was verified to the letter.

Set-backs now began to accumulate on all sides. Between 1633 and 1691 a number of Italian Franciscans were labouring in Abyssinia, more or less secretly, working as slaves and artisans in order to be able to do some missionary work. These seem to have been martyred or to have died in captivity. But in the eighteenth century, the Negus wrote a letter in Greek asking that some new ones might be sent into his country. Three more Franciscans were despatched, but before long they were banished, all except one who was allowed to remain on in order to finish an Arabic translation of the Pentateuch.

In 1639 all Europeans, except the Dutch, were forbidden to enter Japan even for trade, and then only on condition of trampling upon the Cross, a condition which the Hollanders appear to have accepted. This decree came on top of the Japanese martyrdoms of whose victims forty-five were Franciscans. The profession of the Christian faith was not officially sanctioned until the end of the nineteenth century. When French missionaries entered the country at this time, they found large numbers of Japanese still clinging to the faith, in spite of the fact that they had been without priests for nearly two centuries. These, without knowing why, still invoked the name of St. Francis when reciting the *Confiteor* or *I Confess*. "This name," says Padre Gemelli, "was like the sign of a painter at the bottom of a fresco, the colours and contours of which had been obliterated by time and neglect."

Meanwhile, in China, the condemnation of the Rites had

had a most prejudicial effect upon the fortunes of the missions in that country. In 1722, a general persecution broke out under the Emperor Yong-Tschang who published an edict of extermination involving the destruction of more than three hundred churches, the martyrdom of an immense number of Christians (three hundred thousand, it is said) and the expulsion of the missionaries. This edict was not revoked until 1820. During the "closure," the Franciscans and others contrived, by disguising themselves, to run the blockade. Once inside they went underground and, when their converts were carried off to Tartary as slaves, they went with them.

Persecution, bitter and relentless, fell also on the Christian communities in Korea, backed up by the most stringent measures taken to prevent any "strangers" from entering this forbidden land. In the early years of the nineteenth century, a Chinese priest (the one whose coming had been predicted thirty years before) managed to cross the frontier, to be followed soon after by Father Maubant of the French Society of Foreign Missions, and then by Monsignor Imbert, the first Christian bishop who ever set foot among this people so jealous of strangers. He found one thousand Christians in the Korean capital alone, three hundred of whom made their confession to him. The life this prelate was compelled to live in order to avoid detection and arrest makes one of the most heroic stories in the annals of missionary enterprise. He was martyred in 1839.

About the same period, disaster befell the French missions in Indo-China, and that extensive territory also was closed to Europeans and remained so for half a century. Much the same thing happened in Siam, whose Christian history during the eighteenth century is one of persecution and political suppression.

Thanks to the untiring energy of the Jesuits, hopes began to be entertained that all India would be Christianized, but with the suppression of the Society these hopes were dissipated. Shortly before its suppression in 1773, the Society numbered 22,589 members with 669 colleges, 1,542 churches and no fewer than 273 foreign missionary foundations. It seems not unreasonable to infer that, in this last respect, the Jesuits were well ahead of any other single religious Order. At one blow this immense apostolic organization was, not indeed completely destroyed, but certainly ruined for the time being. In places, for example in Maryland, they still continued to labour as private individuals and even to retain their properties; but, in the wide territories where such inveterate enemies of theirs as Spain and Portugal were paramount, the disaster was so overwhelming that it has not been properly retrieved even at the present day. On top of all came the French Revolution and the Napoleonic Wars under the impact of which organized missionary work was practically suspended.

In 1802, the renowned *Société des Missions Etrangères de Paris* mustered only thirty-nine priests for the evangelizing of the extensive mission fields of the East Indies, Indo-China, and China itself. In 1822, out of the five remaining French missions, three were in Indo-China, one in India, one in China; the personnel of these amounted to seven bishops or superiors of Orders, with thirty-nine priests under them. Associated with these were 120 native priests, 400 travelling catechists, and 600 nuns for the needs of 370,000 Christians scattered in the midst of 110 million pagans. Between 1807 and 1816 not a single French priest left for the foreign missions. In 1816 one sailed, in 1818 and 1819 two, both from the diocese of Lyons. Only the skeleton of the missions remained, the bones of which were held together by the catechists who were sorely tried for want of funds. Bonaparte professed to be well-disposed toward the French missions and probably was so, but his ministers would not hear of any subsidies. The most they would allow were a few free berths on board the French ships. This century, the eighteenth, was described by a Frenchman as the least Christian and the least French century in the history of France, and the missions suffered accordingly. Still, as we shall see, the darkest hour of the night is always the one before the dawn.

XXII

SECOND SPRING

IN many respects the nineteenth century is one of the most stimulating periods in the whole history of the Christian apostolate. It was during this time that foreign missionary work began to acquire the features familiar to us at the present day. After the decline and slumber of the wretched eighteenth century, there was an astonishing revival of zeal, and zeal of a very practical kind. Would-be missionaries began to make a careful study of the lie of the land, of local problems, of such hitherto neglected matters as tropical diseases and so on. There were fewer and fewer leaps in the dark. Examples of heroism abounded, heroism as genuine as anything that went before; but those concerned were beginning to realize, what Pope Pius XII was to insist on later, that heroism is not enough. There was a disposition to learn something from the mistakes of the past; in the matter—to give but one example—of fostering native vocations.

Formerly, the Church turned to the old Religious Orders who took up foreign missionary work in conjunction with a multitude of other works. Now we get a whole host of bodies coming into being for this object and for this object alone. A man describing himself as a Jesuit or Dominican may be doing almost anything, from teaching in a University to compiling some monumental literary work. But the term "White Father" suggests a definite context of desert sands, and Arab tents and the burning heat of Africa.

Before the century was over serious attention began to be paid to the problem of providing certain missionary centres with some sort of an organized medical service, and the possibility of founding quasi-religious bodies for that work was beginning to be discussed. Through the heroic self-sacrifice of one man, the conscience of Europe was suddenly roused to concern itself with the plight of the Leper. The Missionary Sister at last came into her own and soon was to be seen, in her thousands, standing up to tasks which had heretofore been thought too arduous or unseemly for her sex.

This reawakened interest in the missions resembled that

which bubbled up in Spain and Portugal in the sixteenth century, with this difference, that the interest was no longer confined to the parties mainly concerned. The business of the world-wide apostolate began to be everybody's business. The gap between laity and clergy was steadily narrowing, and symptoms were appearing of a development that came to be known as Catholic Action. An enthusiasm for, and a desire to help, the missionary undertakings projected or going forward, was one of these symptoms. The veil of mystery which had inevitably surrounded the propagation of the Gospel in far distant lands was drawn aside. Communications between East and West were easier and quicker.

Accounts and reports of activities which, heretofore, had been more or less designed for private circulation were now being publicized by means of reports in the Press, in missionary mazagines and, above all, in the widely-circulated *Annals of the Propagation of the Faith*, which were finding their way into ordinary Catholic homes. The earliest bound volume of these in English, now preserved in the archives of the London headquarters of the Association for the Propagation of the Faith (A.P.F.), dates from May to October 1839, but the first number appeared in France in 1822. It is probably no exaggeration to say that thousands of missionaries owed their vocation, under God, to the reading of these glowing volumes of which one of their number said: "I defy a Christian, worthy of the name, to run over their pages without repeating the words of Clovis on hearing the account of the Passion: 'Why was I not there with my Franks?'" They inspired Father de Bretonnières when, as a small child, he heard them being read in the family. It is said of this missionary, who gave his life for the faith in Korea, that even at that early age he was often found with his ear to the ground and, on being asked what he was doing, replied: "I am listening to the Chinese; they are calling me."

The upshot of all this was that quite ordinary lay-people, especially women, began to roll up their sleeves and to astonish everybody by the soundness of their suggestions, and the intrepidity they displayed in carrying them out. For the necessary finances the missions were no longer content to rely entirely upon royal subsidies. Pauline Jaricot emerged from her obscurity to demonstrate that a million donations of threepence apiece are, after all, equal to a grant of over twelve thousand pounds. Kings and governments, besides, are apt to come and go, whereas the faithful are always with us, and are always the faithful. These facts, and others like them, explain why the nineteenth century has been described as the Popular Epoch of missionary history.

This renaissance was helped along by a number of external circumstances. Among the political ones, there was first of all the changed situation in the Far East. China and Japan not only lifted their Iron Curtains, and opened their doors to the foreigner, but showed a distinct willingness to allow our missionaries to have a free hand. Before it was over, the century was going to see some unfortunate complications in these regions, but at any rate it opened in a favourable and promising atmosphere. In India, the Goan Schism was partly healed, and there was a reconstitution of the hierarchy. The expansion of the French Colonial Empire chimed in with a marked revival of religion in that country. In Europe, Mohammedanism was now politically defunct, or very nearly so, and this meant that certain territories became accessible for the first time in hundreds of years. In 1860, France intervened on behalf of the Christian communities in the Asiatic Near-East, who were menaced by the tyranny of Turks, Arabs and Druses; and, from now on, was the accepted protector of Oriental Christendom, as well as the patron of all missionary undertakings carried on in the Ottoman Empire.

Then, too, the restoration of the Society of Jesus in 1814 took place at a time when the horizon in the Far East was beginning to brighten; and, before long, Jesuit missionaries were returning to the regions consecrated by their earlier labours and successes. They returned to Madura in southern India, the scene of Father de Nobili's bold experiment, in 1838; and, although they no longer dressed like Brahmins, they opened a college to which many of that caste sent their sons; fifty of these young men became Catholics and forfeited their social status in consequence. The Belgian Jesuits took up work in Calcutta and Bengal.

Towards the close of this period, the situation in Africa

was such that its total conversion was being discussed as a not too-remote possibility. With the advent of Islamism it had become, to all intents and purposes, a closed continent, as we have seen. Yet, writing in the middle of the eleventh century, Pope Leo IX was able to express a confident hope that the tide would turn one day. "Carthage," he said, "will keep its canonical primacy so long as the name of Christ shall be invoked within its walls; whether its scanty monuments lie in the dust for ever, as they lie today, or a glorious resurrection shall one day cause these ruins to rise again." Sure enough, in the nineteenth century Africa was so far from being a Mohammedan preserve that the European powers were leisurely and systematically dividing it up among themselves. By the end of the century, the whole of its vast coast line had passed into the possession of Christian powers.

This turn of events enabled the missionaries to move in, and they did move in to some purpose. French, Italians, English, Spaniards, Irish, Portuguese, Germans—all nationalities were represented among them. When the republic of Liberia was being set up three Irish missionaries from America started a mission there which was later taken over by the Holy Ghost Fathers. This was the beginning of a revival which made such headway that, before long, it was not easy to find a single area along the shores washed by the Mediterranean, the Atlantic and the Indian Ocean untouched by the apostolate.

It was, of course, otherwise with the interior of the Dark Continent. This had hitherto appeared to be almost inaccessible. Then came the discoveries of Livingstone, Stanley and Speke, and these paved the way for an outburst of missionary energy in that direction. Towards the end of his Pontificate, Pope Pius IX directed those in charge of the various African missionary societies to put their heads together, and formulate some plan for the conquest of Equatorial Africa. At the same time, concerted efforts were made by speech and pen to rouse the European powers into action against the iniquity of the Mohammedan slave-trade which, in certain regions, was the great obstacle standing in the missionary's path.

Whereas Protestantism had for long left the missionary

field severely alone, it now began to direct its energies to this branch of religious activity. Frederick IV of Denmark founded a missionary college in 1714. The Moravians, or United Brethren, who trace their origin to John Huss, were expelled from their original home but settled in Saxony, and began to take up missionary work with conspicuous energy, especially in Greenland. Their example was soon followed elsewhere; so that, at the end of the nineteenth century, there were reckoned to be seventy Protestant missionary societies in existence, forty-five of which were in Great Britain and North America. Their agents began to appear in every part of the world, and they met with conspicuous success in Polynesia, South and West Africa, and in Madagascar. Although they were late in entering China, by the end of the century there were eighty-two bodies working there, a number of whose members were medical missionaries. During this century, the British and Foreign Bible Society printed and distributed eighteen million copies of the Scriptures, translated into three hundred and twenty-four languages.

It would be idle to deny that this intervention was a source of embarrassment to the old timers. It was and still is; in many places, Lazarus found it difficult to compete with Dives. At the same time, to say nothing of the competitive element introduced, there was something to be learned from the methods these bodies employed for promoting their beliefs. The importance they attached to medical work, and the success of their exertions in this direction, were not without effect upon those who are sometimes over-anxious to keep jogging along in "the good old way."

The achievements of the century may be briefly summarized as follows. At its beginning, there were in India 475,000 Catholics and at the end 1,700,000. Indo-China—which included Burma, Cambodia, Cochin-China, Siam, Malacca and Tonkin—had 319,000 in 1800 and over a million in 1900. The Catholic population of China in 1900 was estimated at a million, whereas in 1800 there were only 200,000 faithful in five mission-centres. As late as 1860 there were, as far as anyone knew, no Catholics at all in Japan, while in 1900 the figure given was 60,000. In the whole of North Africa, one hundred years ago, there were no more than 15,000 Catholics. In the eastern part there was only one bishopric with eight or ten priests.

And this nineteenth century, so generous in every way, furnished its generous quota of martyrdoms; individual ones in most of the mission fields and, in certain places, large-scale holocausts reminiscent of the early centuries. Always the root cause of the trouble was the same—an antipathy to the European whom the native races, almost everywhere, had only too many reasons for regarding as Enemy Number One. For all his single-mindedness and detachment, the missionary cannot help carrying his nationality with him wherever he goes. He may dress like an African arab, a Chinese bonze or an Indian brahmin—and missionaries have figured in the dress of all three—but his identity can never be properly concealed, or concealed for long. Inevitably, therefore, whenever fear and hatred of foreign domination comes to a head among primitive peoples, the first to suffer will be those who are suspected of being the accomplices of that domination.

Thus it was in Indo-China where the French had founded many flourishing missions during this century. The cruelties practised by the Portuguese in the sixteenth century had, however, left very unpleasant memories behind, and the monarch who came to the throne as Emperor of Annam in 1820 issued edicts the object of which was to chase the European out of the country and, in consequence, to extinguish the Christian faith. These edicts were the prelude to a persecution, known as the Great Massacres, only brought to an end when Annam became a French protectorate some sixty years later.

The mission of Uganda in the Upper Nile also had its baptism of blood. The White Fathers entered this territory in 1878 and laboured in peace for some years. But, in 1886, the Arabs began to work upon the fears of King Mwanga. A persecution ensued in which a native Christian, the chief of the royal pages, was the first to suffer death. He was followed by more than one hundred others.

When the century drew to its close, China was swarming with missionaries of various nationalities who were known to be, and made no secret of the fact that they were, foreigners. In 1898, an agitation against the foreigner started up in the

Celestial Empire, or, at any rate, in certain parts of it. Its members belonged to what was called the League of United Patriots; but, since they went in for athletics, the Americans nicknamed them Boxers. The movement culminated in the Boxer Rising of 1899, during which large numbers of innocent people were put to death under circumstances of marked brutality. The promoters of the persecution unscrupulously played upon the fears of the simple Chinese people, suggesting —among other things—that the reason why the missionaries were collecting the orphans and abandoned babies into their homes was that they might use their eyes for manufacturing the "elixir of life." All nationalities suffered. No fewer than thirty-six bishops were martyred, the majority of whom were either French, Dutch, Italian or Belgian.

XXIII

FRANCE IN THE ASCENDANT

IN this enthusiastic revival, and under all its aspects, the primacy of France was unquestionable. That country had hardly recovered from the prolonged shock and demoralization of the Revolution when it began to display an amazing fertility in the production of missionary vocations. At the end of the century, a table was drawn up showing the number of missionaries of French nationality actually working abroad, along with the titles of the Religious Orders (thirty-five in all) to which they belonged. Many of these Orders were new bodies instituted for foreign-missionary purposes alone. The *Société des Missions Etrangères* heads the list with twelve hundred, while the Brothers of the Christian Schools are a good second with eight hundred and thirteen.

Taking one of the new bodies at random, we find that the Oblates of Mary Immaculate came into existence in 1816. Before very long its members were to be found in Ceylon, in Natal and the Transvaal and among the Zulus, Basutos, Bechuanas and Kaffirs. In Canada, "they braved the rapids of the Red River, the Mackenzie, the Saskatchewan and the Athabaska; they climbed the dizzy heights of the Rockies; they trailed over the endless snow-fields and ice-lakes to win to the faith the fierce Indian tribes and the Eskimos."

To the total of 7,745 religious men given in the aforesaid table must be added nearly a thousand women of various Congregations supplied by France alone. This is not a large number in comparison with modern statistics; but, in the absence of figures, it is fairly safe to say that at no time during the sixteenth and seventeenth centuries was a comparable number of missionaries at work in the whole of the American continent, not the least striking feature of whose conversion is the fewness of the agents employed.

This French personnel was distributed over a wide area, with a notable concentration of effort on the Near East where the baneful effects of the Moslem occupation had to be counteracted, and the various dissident bodies won back to the unity of the faith. In the Far East, French missionaries were to be found in Ceylon, India, Burma, Siam, Korea, Tonkin, Cochin-China, China proper and Japan. In China they maintained the cultural traditions handed down from the sixteenth and seventeenth centuries. They published a French-Korean dictionary, besides works on philology and natural science.

Frenchmen were labouring at this time in the islands scattered between Japan and New Zealand. Catholic missions to that world of islands known as Oceania date from the year 1837, when Father Bataillon landed on Wallis Island with nothing but a cross to protect him from the cannibals. In this region, the rage for human flesh was such that members of the same tribes hunted and ate one another. One missionary reported at this time that Mass was being regularly said in the hut of a king who, not long before, had as many as fourteen men served up piping hot at his breakfast table. The French continued to labour in this area for years, Father Bataillon being made a bishop.

In 1832 two French priests opened in Madagascar the mission that had been abandoned one hundred and fifty years before. Great difficulties were experienced here owing to the opposition of the Queen. It was not until her successor ascended the throne that real progress could be made. Chapels and schools were built, and a cathedral erected in the capital. In 1883 the converted natives amounted to eighty thousand.

In spite of a prolonged persecution, French missionaries stuck to their posts in Indo-China. During the "Great Massacres," as they were called, the mission properties were destroyed and thousands of native Christians put to death, as well as scores of priests, many of them natives. Before the end of the century, however, the Church in Indo-China was in a fair way to become one of the most prosperous in the Far East, thanks to the energy of its French bishops, backed up by a host of French missionary organizations. The converts amounted to very nearly a million.

When, after labouring for thirty-five years and making numerous converts, the Capuchin Fathers were driven from Tibet, no missionary (as far as is known) suceeded in entering that country until 1846 when two French Lazarists, Fathers Huc and Gabet, reached Lhasa. Their journey was one of indescribable difficulty and lasted for eighteen months. Never did a missionary undertaking commence under more favourable auspices. A chapel was fitted up in the palace of the Regent, the Gospel began to be publicly expounded by the lamas, and the cross was worn publicly on the necks of the Christian converts. At the end of three months, unfortunately, the Chinese envoy in Tibet so wrought upon the Regent that he was compelled to send the two priests out of the country. Nothing daunted by this failure, a succession of attempts was made by French missionaries to establish themselves in the forbidden land. They came to nothing, it is true, but the French have never to this day abandoned the hope of being able to evangelize the metropolis of the Buddhist world.

In Africa generally, and in Central Africa especially, French energy was conspicuous. Father Libermann, a converted Alsatian Jew, founded or reorganized a missionary body whose subjects are said to have been the first, in modern times, to penetrate to the interior of the continent. The members of this body are known as the Holy Ghost Fathers and their activities, at the present day, in Africa alone cover nearly thirty missionary territories. The missionaries themselves number over three thousand—not counting the Sisters—of whom thirty-two are bishops.

About twenty years after the establishment of this Society, France sent to Africa a man who was destined to become the greatest champion its people ever had. Charles Lavigerie was made Archbishop of Algiers in 1867. On landing, he remarked to those about him: "I shall not seek one day's rest"; and he kept his word. "Algiers", he wrote at this time, "is only the threshold of a continent with more than two hundred millions of inhabitants; their conversion must be the ultimate aim of all our efforts." The first thing this "parish-priest of half a continent" did was to reverse the policy of neutrality towards the Moslems imposed upon his predecessor by the French authorities. Realizing that the Christian future of Africa was bound up with their conversion, he founded the Society of Missionaries of Africa.

The clergy he had in his archdiocese had been trained in the ordinary way to do the ordinary work of parochial priests. None of them had learned Arabic nor yet any of the

African dialects. But since this new Society of his purposed, as its main object, to bring the Mohammedans under the influence of the Gospel, he dressed his White Fathers in the *grandura*, *burnus*, red-cap and rosary of the North African Arab. He set his face against all attempts to Europeanize the natives, and he forbade his missionaries to teach them to read and write French. Some missionaries had been inclined to deny the possibility of converting the Mohammedans. Lavigerie would not accept that, but he had no illusions as to the difficulty of the thing. He warned his associates that a prolonged and patient period of preparation would be necessary, before any tangible results could be expected, and it was twenty years before he would allow even one Arab to be baptized.

But the success among the Africans of the interior has been outstanding. In 1878, Leo XIII created four extensive missionary Vicariates in the region of the equatorial lakes, Nyanza, Tanganyika and two in Upper Congo. These were handed over to the White Fathers, ten of whom set out in March of the same year. The starting point was Zanzibar, the focus of all African exploration. In July the caravan reached the mountainous district of Usagura. Here, repeated attacks of fever began to tell on the party, one of whom, the priest in charge, succumbed after a few weeks' illness—the first to lay down his life for the salvation of the negro. Within a few years, three of the pioneers sent to Lake Tanganyika were killed by the arrows of the Urundi. Their places were filled by others, with the result that this unpromising field was producing phenomenal harvests. In 1922 there were fourteen thousand Christians in this district, and in 1939 the figure had risen to three hundred and twenty-five thousand. Nor is there any sign of this mass-movement slowing down, for recent statistics give more than forty thousand baptisms for one year, with a waiting-list of catechumens amounting to eighty-four thousand. All this has happened in a territory no bigger than Holland and carrying a population of only two million.

Meanwhile, the missions served by the White Fathers and White Sisters have prospered to such a degree that they now have charge of some thirty districts containing two and a half million baptized, and over three quarters of a million catechumens. The priests of the society number nearly two thousand, of whom three hundred and fifty-seven are native priests. About two thousand Sisters and five hundred Brothers figure in their statistics, along with twelve thousand five hundred catechists.

Missionary work in Africa was hampered, from the start, by peculiar difficulties which Cardinal Lavigerie reviewed in a letter written to the Society for the Propagation of the Faith. He pointed out that, although Mohammedanism was dying out in Europe, it was making rapid progress among the natives of Africa, being imposed upon them by force. Polygamy was another obstacle, as well as a certain indifference to religion which, at that time at any rate, was noticeable among the Negroes. But Lavigerie exerted the full weight of his eloquence against the slave-trade, carried on by the Mussulmans, which he called upon the European powers to use their influence to suppress.

In spite of the fact that France was not a rich country, the bulk of the money collected for missionary causes came from her people. Just as a woman had played a conspicuous part in the founding and development of the *Société des Missions Etrangères*, so now the world-famous Association for the Propagation of the Faith was to owe its inspiration to another woman, this time at the other end of the social scale. Pauline Jaricot invented this remarkable machine, which no longer astonishes us simply because its workings are now familiar. The plan was hers and she directed its first operations in person. "I realized," she said, "how easily each person of my own intimate circle could find ten other persons, including herself, who would each give a half-penny. In order to simplify the association, each leader of a thousand persons would refer to a common centre. I wrote out my plan at once for fear of forgetting it. It astonished me that no one had thought of such a simple scheme before."

The actual foundation was in 1819. At the end of a year about 23,000 francs had been collected; at the end of five years more than 100,000 francs. By 1838 the Association was known all over the world, and subscriptions were sent from the United States, from Austria and Spain; when, in 1840, South America joined in, 2,000,000 francs were subscribed.

In 1842 the sum amounted to 3,233,000, half of which was collected in France alone. From that time onwards the subscriptions went on increasing. In 1919 they reached fifteen millions, and again in 1920 fifteen millions. The total receipts of the Association during the hundred years of its existence amount to 500,000,000 francs.

The Association was reorganized on a national basis in England in 1839 when its contributions rose from £95 in 1837 to £1,596. In 1950 the total receipts for England and Wales amounted to over £50,000.

The Society of the Holy Childhood was founded in 1843 by the Bishop of Nancy, and organized in Great Britain by the wife of Ambrose Phillipps de Lisle. Every year it is instrumental in the regeneration of half a million infants, snatched either from death or from slavery, and educated in orphanages and special schools. These schools are recruiting-grounds for native vocations. This work for children is, to a big extent, financed by children, since a branch of the Society is to be found in most of our convent and parochial schools.

We may note, too, that in 1838 a French woman, Marie du Chesne, formed a group of workers whose aim was to supply the foreign missions with altar furnishings and things of that kind, an enterprise destined to be imitated in other countries later on.

A lesser-known French undertaking belonging to this period owed its existence to the enthusiasm and generosity of two French laymen. In a previous chapter, something was said of the difficulties French missionaries experienced in finding ships to convey them to their destinations. In the beginning of the year 1845, there was established at Havre a maritime society, the object of which was to provide this necessary transport, as well as to insure the missions against any failure of material resources. The idea originated with the Vicar Apostolic of New Caledonia, and was taken up warmly by a merchant of Havre and an officer in the French navy. The former purchased a large ship, then building in the port of Nantes, and the latter undertook to command it. It was blessed by the Bishop and dedicated to Mary under the title of the *Arche d'Alliance* (Ark of the Covenant); and, on November 15th, 1845, it sailed from the port of Havre for

11

the islands of western Oceania. When Christmas came, Midnight Mass was said on deck. Instead of taking the usual route and doubling Cape Horn, the vessel steered its course towards the Straits of Magellan. Landing on the island of St. Elizabeth, the crew and passengers placed Patagonia under the protection of the Cross and the Immaculate Virgin. Later they reached a small Spanish colony on the mainland where they found an Italian Franciscan in charge. He had not seen a priest for eighteen months. In *Tierra del Fuego* (Land of Fire) they erected a cross thirty-five feet high on the spot nearest to the South Pole.

When the time came for a fresh batch of French missionaries to set out for their destination, everything was done to make the occasion a memorable one. The grounds and chapel of the Training College were thrown open to the public, and in this way interest in the missions and missionary vocations was fostered.

Among the collection of Essays to which he gave the name of *La Belle Souffrance*, François Coppée has one in which he describes the impression made upon himself by this ceremony. The first part of it took place in the garden in a corner of which stood a statue of our Blessed Lady surrounded by lighted candles. The *Partants* knelt before it chanting the Litany of Loreto. Their heads were bowed, but from where he stood he could see the white nape of their necks "bent as if offering themselves to the blade of the executioner." The final act was the most touching of all, the farewell. "Their feet were kissed to wish them a good journey and a prosperous harvest among the heathen, and their cheeks in token of brotherly affection and an eternal *adieu*."

As to the feelings of the *Partants* themselves, something may be learned from the letter which Théophane Venard wrote to his sister on the eve of going to Tonkin and to his death.

"Yes I know well the sorrow I am going to bring upon my family and especially upon you, my darling sister. But don't you realize that it cost me tears of blood, too, to take such a step, and give you all such pain? Who ever cared more for home and for home-life than I? All my happiness here below was centred in it. What a fight and a struggle I have had with my poor human nature."

XXIV

ALL-ROUND EFFORTS

IT is not suggested that France monopolized the apostolate at this time. In various parts of the world, continuity with the past continued to be maintained by subjects of the great pioneering nations, Spain and Portugal. The division of Africa among the European powers naturally meant that this or that annexed territory would be evangelized by missionaries belonging to the country concerned. Belgian priests went into the Belgian Congo, and Germans followed their compatriots into Togoland, the Cameroons and Damarland. Indeed, the predominance of France is, to a large extent, explained by the fact of her colonial expansion, just as the predominance of Spain or Portugal in the missions of the sixteenth and seventeenth centuries is explained by the expansion of these countries in that period. It is only within recent years that Italy began to have colonies at all, and this may account for the relatively poor contribution she made to the work of the apostolate in distant parts.

Notwithstanding this obvious political handicap, there was, outside France, a marked reawakening of interest during the nineteenth century. In Italy itself, the Pallottine Fathers were founded in 1835, the Milan Foreign Missionaries in 1850, the Salesians in 1855, the Verona Fathers in 1867, the Institute of St. Francis Xavier of Parma in 1895 and the Missionaries of the Consolata in 1900. The Claretians began in Spain in 1848 and the Mill Hill Fathers in England in 1866; while Germany gave us the Society of the Divine Word, the Salvatorians and the Missionary Society of St. Benedict.

Even the Catholics of Holland began to assert themselves, in spite of the fact that their emancipation only came about in the middle of this century. By the end of it, they had some two dozen colleges in which missionaries were being trained for Borneo, the Dutch East and West Indies, Brazil, Porto Rico and the Philippines. The Society of the Servants of the Holy One was founded in 1889. This crusade eventually brought Holland right to the front as a missionary nation.

Much might be said, and in justice ought to be said, of

these new organizations, as also of those noticed in the previous chapter. Each one has grown and grown, from a small beginning and through the tribulations inseparable from supernatural efforts here below, to the stature familiar to us at the present day. Each lives and thrives on the memory of a saintly founder (Vincent Pallotti and Anthony Mary Claret were canonized during the Holy Year of 1950), bringing his project to completion in the face of oppositions and obstacles; or, it may be, being snatched away, by death or by other duties, from participation in the work upon which he had set his heart. There seems no doubt, for example, that Herbert Vaughan ardently desired, not only to establish a missionary college, but also to labour in the missionary field. The first part of his ambition was realized, but not the second. All these undertakings have, too, their roll of honour inscribed with the names of the pioneers whose sole contribution to the cause was the early sacrifice of their young lives in the far-distant lands which they had so yearned to evangelize.

Here again, however, a glimpse in passing is about all that the scope of this book permits us to have of these multiple organizations. We may linger for a moment over the Society of the Divine Word because it was the first German missionary society to be established. It is sometimes referred to as Steyl from the Dutch town in which it originated, during the Kulturkampf, in 1875. The founder, Father Arnold Janssen, also created an association of religious women to work with the Society. In less than ten years a start was made in Shantung, China. A second mission was opened in West Africa and a third in New Guinea among the Papuans. In this last-named territory, the missionaries had to contend with more than a hundred different languages spoken within a radius of less than five hundred miles. In 1898 work was begun in a district of South America, part of which includes the site of the Jesuit Reductions of Paraguay. Equally rapid was the progress of the Salvatorians, another German organization of religious men and women. Today this Society has over seventy houses, although it was started only in 1881. The founder, Father Jordan, was inspired in the first place by the text: "This is eternal life: that they may know Thee, the only true God, and Jesus Christ whom Thou hast sent."

Nor did the uprising of these new apostolic bodies mean that the older Religious Orders had ceased to pull their weight. The oldest of all, the Benedictines, were actively employed in Ceylon, in western Bengal, in North America among the Indians, in New Zealand, in the Argentine and, eventually, in the Transvaal. In 1845 they began work among the aborigines of Australia by opening a settlement not unlike the Jesuit Reductions. They called it New Nursia after the Perugian birthplace of their founder, and this linked it up with their primitive past. From this centre, two Spaniards successfully evangelized the western part of the continent. The Congregation of St. Ottilien was established for the express purpose of providing missionaries, and to these were entrusted ten mission stations in the Vicariate of Zanzibar. The Brazilian Congregation has several missions in Brazil, and the Cistercians, who profess the Benedictine Rule, in Natal.

Individual Franciscans were very much to the fore in Africa, and it was partly owing to their zeal that the missions were reorganized in Peru, Chile and Bolivia. Australia and New Zealand were visited by Italian Franciscans as early as the latter part of the seventeenth century, and in 1878 their places were filled by members of the Irish province. At the end of the century, there were five thousand friars working in five continents and assisted by 12,500 Franciscan Sisters. In China, Japan, Peru, Brazil, Cuba, Dominicans continued their efforts, and broke new ground by entering the Belgian Congo. In spite of the misfortunes that had fallen upon their Order, the Jesuits, as we have seen, began to find their way back to their old posts.

Countess Maria Ledóchowska, the Mother of the Africans, was a native of Austria whose vocation came to her when it was least expected. She was performing her duties as lady-in-waiting to the Archduchess of Tuscany when two missionary Sisters visited the palace in Salzburg on a collecting tour. The conversation that followed served as Maria's introduction to the needs and problems of the foreign missions. Twelve months later, two other Sisters, intent on the same errand, visited the palace, one of whom was Countess de Gélin, formerly a lady-in-waiting at the same Court. The example of this woman's renunciation deepened still further the impression made by the first interview. Then a Protestant friend sent her a booklet treating of Cardinal Lavigerie and his crusade against the African slave-trade. She began to read it, and came upon the following extract from a speech he had delivered in London:

"Christian women of Europe, you are in duty bound to expose these infamies. Let those to whom God has given ability to write consecrate their pen to this holy cause. Do not forget that it was the work of a woman, the novel *Uncle Tom's Cabin*, that sealed the doom of American slavery."

Maria began by contributing some articles on the African Missions to a periodical. She followed this up by starting a periodical of her own entitled *The Echo From Africa*. Subscribers and contributions grew rapidly. Next she compiled the rules of an association called the Sodality of St. Peter Claver for the African Missions. In the first house of this Institute established near Salzburg she set up a polyglot printing press. At the time of her death, in 1922, the Sodality had houses or dependencies in many parts of the world, had already contributed twelve and a half million lire to the cause, and could rely upon the support of fifty thousand promoters and five hundred thousand associates. One of her favourite activities was the provision of literature for the natives; and, within the space of twenty years, her Institute had forwarded to Africa very nearly two hundred thousand books written in nineteen languages. She lived to see her organization instrumental in the freeing of about sixteen thousand slaves.

Father Damien (Joseph de Veuster) was born at Tremeloo, Belgium, in 1840 and died of leprosy at the age of forty-eight. He was ordained priest, at Honolulu, as a member of the Congregation of Picpus. In 1873, at his own request, he took up his residence in the leper settlement on the island of Molokai, Hawaii, to care for the stricken inmates who, at that time, had neither resident physician, nurse nor chaplain. For twelve years he laboured alone at the task of ministering to their physical and spiritual needs, even to the extent of making their coffins and burying their dead. In 1885 he discovered on himself the symptoms of that dread disease, but he remained at his post, nevertheless, until his decease three years later. If Damien's fame had not been spread by other witnesses, it would have been kept alive by the remonstrance which R. L. Stevenson addressed to the Rev. Dr. Hyde who had attacked the character of the priest.

The news of what Damien had been doing spread, and attention began to be paid to the plight of the world's lepers of whom there are said to be at least three million (some say seven million). Of these there are proportionately more in Africa than in any other country; five hundred thousand is the figure given for British Africa alone. This immense problem will not be solved, or anything like solved, until scores, nay hundreds, of medical missionary bodies are created for the express purpose. As it is, most of the work being done for these afflicted creatures is being done by missionaries of various denominations. Catholic societies are caring for twelve thousand of them in one hundred and eight leprosariums. Ireland's great modern enterprise, the Medical Missionaries of Mary, had founded a leper colony in Nigeria before it had been a dozen years in existence. In this district there are now three settlements in working order, with nearly three thousand patients on the registers.

For a long time now, the Franciscan Missionaries of Mary have been particularly active in this field, and an association was formed in England with the object of assisting their work. Called the St. Francis Leper Guild, it owed its origin to Miss Kate Marsden, a Franciscan Tertiary, who, having travelled in the East, was horrified by the conditions she saw there. She promised God to spend the rest of her life, first in trying to find a cure for the disease and, failing that, in devising ways and means of alleviating the miseries of the lepers and of bringing them under the influence of the Gospel. The first meeting took place in London in 1895 at which a sum of £67 was collected. Since then the Guild has distributed over £60,000 to leper colonies all over the world.

On March 19th, 1866, the first Foreign Missionary College in Great Britain was formally opened at Mill Hill. This venture, which started off with one priest and one student, owed almost everything to Herbert Vaughan who later became Cardinal Archbishop of Westminster. Mill Hill was the great passion of his life. He ended his days there, and the simple tombstone in its cemetery bears the inscription "Herbert Vaughan, Missionary." In the end he offered his life as a sacrifice to God if, at the expense of his death, He would establish in England a seminary for Foreign Missions. Each time he tried to put the project on one side, he lost his peace of mind. "In such tribulation of soul was born the Missionary Society of Mill Hill."

In order to raise the necessary funds Herbert Vaughan resolved to turn beggar, and he chose South America as the field of his operations. A generous benefactor was Lady Herbert of Lea who thus earned for herself the title of "The Mother of the Mill."

The first duty entrusted to the new body was among the negroes of the United States. A few years after, they made themselves responsible for a portion of the diocese of Madras. Mill Hill priests have been working in north-west India for over sixty years. Four of them set out for Afghanistan in 1879, and later the Society took over the Prefecture of Kashmir and Kafristan as well as that of North Borneo. When nearly all the Spanish missionaries had to quit the Philippines on their occupation by America in 1898, eight Mill Hill Fathers left for Manila. The first band reached New Zealand in 1886 and began work among the Maoris. The next call brought the Society into Uganda to which territory there has been a constant flow of missionaries ever since. Today there are over two hundred and twenty thousand Catholics in the Vicariate with one hundred and thirty priests in charge. Out of this mission grew the one of Kisumu in Kenya Colony. For all these territories, which now include the Cameroons and the Anglo-Egyptian Sudan, there are about eight hundred priests available; while over six hundred students are being educated for the priesthood in a number of colleges, three of which are in England, three in Holland, one in Italy and one in Austria.

Great as were the services rendered to Africa by Cardinal Lavigerie they must not be allowed to obscure those of the Italian Cardinal Massaia, who laboured in Abyssinia for thirty-five years. Each time he visited Europe he interviewed government departments in the endeavour to interest them in the welfare, spiritual and temporal, of its inhabitants. He introduced vaccination against smallpox into Abyssinia and established medical clinics. His work was carried on by others, notably by Vito Fornari, a Capuchin.

Another great-hearted "African" was the Italian Father Daniel Comboni, the founder of the Verona Fathers, whose motto was "Either Africa or Death." The determination to become a foreign missionary came to him when, at the age of fifteen, he happened to read an account of the Martyrs of Japan. His first Mass was a solemn dedication of his life to the work of the African missions. He was twenty-eight years of age when, with five companions, he reached the mission station of the Holy Cross more than a thousand miles up the Nile from Khartoum. Within the year, four of the priests had succumbed to tropical fever and the two survivors returned to Europe. But Comboni did not give in. His motto summed up all his ideals and aspirations. Before many years, he had launched his *Plan for the Regeneration of Africa*, had founded his first missionary college in Verona and was back in Africa organizing his campaign. At this time he made the acquaintance of the explorer Stanley, and of General Gordon, then at Khartoum. On the eve of the Mahdist revolution, he sickened and died at the age of fifty. Today his sons (The Verona Fathers) have centres in the Sudan, Uganda, Eritrea, Egypt and Mozambique, as well as in California and Mexico.

If the sight of a map of Africa upset Herbert Vaughan, that of the Asiatic continent had the same effect on Don Bosco. Occupied though he was at home with a multitude of tasks, he was resolved to carry his apostolate into the missionary field at the first opportunity. The opportunity presented itself in the form of a vision, which he himself described as follows:

"It seemed to me that I was in a vast and desolate plain over which a large number of people were running. They were almost naked, very tall and savage-looking, with bristling hair and black-hued skin. They were armed with long spears and something that looked like slings. Then I saw that a number of persons whom I recognized as Christian missionaries were wandering across the plain, and beginning to preach Christianity to these savages. It was not long, however, before the savages attacked them, dismembered the bodies and carried the blood-dripping remains in triumph on their spears. At this sight I asked myself: how are these terrible people ever to be converted? At the same moment, I saw a new company of missionaries coming forward and approaching the savages. They were Salesian priests and students. I saw that the savages did them no harm and went smilingly to meet our people. The missionaries were now able to teach them, instruct and admonish them; and, at last, all the savages threw away their weapons and fell on their knees. One of the Salesians stood in the middle and in a loud voice began to sing a hymn to Mary. All the savages joined in it, until at length the singing grew so loud that it wakened me up."

This happened in 1870. It was not until four years had passed that Don Bosco was able to discover the identity and whereabouts of these savages. He rummaged about among atlases and books treating of ethnology, in the meantime, but without success. In 1874 the Argentine consul called on him with a request that he should send some of his priests and brothers to work in Patagonia. On being shown some pictures of the natives, he at once recognized the savages of his dream. What he had taken for slings turned out to be their lassoes.

Within twelve months, the first band had set out for Argentina, ten in all. The ten had increased to fifteen hundred in the course of the next fifty years, and the original Patagonian mission had thrown out branches into Tierra del Fuego, Brazil, Ecuador and Paraguay. "From the primeval forests along La Plata and the Amazon," writes Jörgensen in his *Life of Don Bosco*, "the Salesians have gone over to the primeval forests of Africa, along the Congo and further eastwards, to Egypt and Palestine, to India, Siam and China and to Japan, closing up the chain now stretching from one coast of the Pacific, round the world, to the other. Altogether 925 missionaries, rather more than 400 Sisters and about 560 native catechists labour in these immense fields. And about 650 young people at home in the mission schools are waiting for their turn to go out and take part in the work."

By 1934, the disciples of Don Bosco had one hundred and twenty-seven houses in Asia and Africa alone, thirty of these being the establishments appertaining to the religious women associated with his work. Today in the same area there are one hundred and seventy-two foundations. Apropos of Don Bosco's vision, it is interesting to note that the Salesian church recently (1949) erected in Tierra del Fuego has the distinction of being the nearest Catholic place of worship to the South Pole. Before he died, the Saint bequeathed to his sons and daughters the world over the following Missionary Testament:

"Seek to gain souls: do not seek money or honours or high positions. Above all care for the sick, for the poor, for children and the aged. Avoid idleness and strife among yourselves. Show respect to all persons in authority. Do not criticize other missionaries. Let your poverty be evident to all men. Keep the rule of our Order; in particular, do not omit the monthly remembrance of death and the preparation for a good death. In all sufferings and trials, remember that an exceeding great reward is laid up for us in heaven."

XXV

MISSIONARY SISTERS

CARDINAL LAVIGERIE insisted that the efforts of the missionaries, in Africa at any rate, would be entirely unsuccessful unless and until apostolic women in large numbers came forward, and began to play a real part in the work of evangelization. Nuns were required there in particular, not only for the works of charity that needed to be done but also, and above all, for the sake of the moral and social influence of their mere presence. The degradation of women in Africa was, geographically, almost a total degradation. Among the Mohammedans, the movement of emancipation was still a long way off, and their unwholesome traditions were unchallenged. It was their idea that women were created for one purpose only, and that anything other than a rigid subordination amounting to servitude was unsuited to their sex. It was necessary to let them see what women could become, and had become, under the influence of a different set of ideas. Their own women were what Mahomet, the Unclean Prophet, had made them; the Missionary Sister represented an earlier creation, Christ's creation in fact. The thing was to bring the two creations face to face; alongside the sexual slave and plaything, to place the product of the Incarnation with all its prestige, dignity and nobility.

The same sort of lesson had to be learned by the Blacks, among whom the lot of a woman was a desperate one. From cradle to grave she was and remained a piece of property; the property of her father first of all, who in due course would sell her to the highest bidder. In the event of her husband's death, she and her children reverted to his heir who could either marry or sell her. She was the breadwinner; and, the richer her toil made her husband, the more wives he was able to buy, so that at last she became one of an ever-expanding harem.

Although there are close upon seventy thousand nuns now employed in Foreign Missionary work, it was not until the middle of the nineteenth century that it was deemed expedient to make full use of women in this way. We may recall how Boniface brought some Anglo-Saxon nuns over to Germany, where they opened schools for the education of girls, besides devoting themselves to the service of the sick. At an early date, besides the usual convents, educational establishments for girls were opened in the New World, and we are informed that twelve "women teachers" came over from Spain to superintend one of them. In the seventeenth century, four nuns and a novice belonging to the Second Order of Dominicans at Marseilles went to Martinique, and founded a convent the inmates of which were required to assist the friars in all their works of charity, in so far as such assistance was compatible with their cloistered life.

We have spoken already of the Duchesse d'Aiguillon, Cardinal Richelieu's niece, and of her zeal for the missions. She was particularly interested in Canada, and she co-operated in planning the foundation of the colony of Montreal. On the first of August 1639, some French Ursulines landed in Quebec and proceeded to erect the first educational establishment for women in North America. This enterprise was financed by the Duchess. The first Mother Superior, Marie de l'Incarnation, compiled dictionaries, a manual of church-history and a catechism in the Algonquin and Iroquois languages. It was in the chapel of this convent that Montcalm was buried after Wolfe's victory in 1759. Two or three years after their arrival, some Hospital Sisters from Dieppe took charge of the *Hôtel-Dieu* in the same city.

When the nineteenth century came, this sort of thing was no longer a novelty, and small groups of nuns, belonging to various Orders, were unobtrusively making their way into heathen lands. The Dominican Sisters of Langres made foundations in China and in Tonkin. In 1822, Mère Javouhey, the foundress of the Congregation of St. Joseph of Cluny who was beatified in 1950, established a house at Gorée in West Africa; and, six years after that, she set out for Guiana with thirty-six nuns, to work among the negroes there. In 1866, some Dominican Sisters of the Third Order went from Châlons to Trinidad as missionary helpers, with special attention paid to the lepers. Rose-Philippine Duchesne who founded the first houses of the Sacred Heart Congregation in North America went, in her old age, to Sugar Creek, the headquarters of the Potawatamy Indians. Franciscan nuns volunteered for missionary work in the Gran Chaco of South America in 1864. About this same time, two French Mission-ary Congregations came into being, the Sisters of the Immaculate Conception and the Daughters of St. Francis de Sales; the first of these chose Africa as the field of its operations, while the second concentrated on India and Madagascar. A Congregation of women called the Franciscan Missionaries of Egypt began to work in Cairo, about the middle of the century, and later spread through Northern Africa and the Holy Land; while, during the Pontificate of Leo XIII, and at his sugges-tion, Anna Lapini, the foundress of the Stimmatine, sent six of her Sisters to Albania to open a school.

So far, however, efforts of this kind were haphazard and unorganized, and the volunteers lacked the specialized training necessary to ensure success. In 1877, therefore, Pope Pius IX entrusted the foundation of a Missionary Training College to a French lady, Helène Chappotin de Neuville, whose name, when she took the veil, became Mère Marie de la Passion. She it was who created the Institute of the Franciscan Missionaries of Mary. Her aim was to create an organization which would give sufficient moral and technical preparation for work on the Foreign Missions. During their noviciate, the Sisters were required to learn printing, poultry-keeping, agriculture, sewing and other things which would be of practical use to them on the Mission. Heléne and her first companions were enrolled as Franciscan Tertiaries in the Church of the Ara Coeli in Rome in 1882. These Sisters were to concentrate chiefly on China and India. Before the Com-munists began their systematic liquidation of the missions in the 1950's, the Franciscan Missionaries of Mary had fifty-six convents in China alone; besides schools, orphanages, welfare-centres, hospitals, leper-asylums, dispensaries and homes for the aged. Their foundations in Asia (including China), Oceania, Africa and South America amount to two hundred and thirty-eight.

Since the inception of this enterprise, institutes of a similar kind have come into being in such numbers that, to furnish even a bare catalogue of them, would make a serious demand upon the space at our disposal. Almost all the missionary

Congregations of men now work in conjunction with affiliated bodies of missionary women. The White Fathers and White Sisters have been in active co-operation for many years. The Sisters of the Holy Ghost, who collaborate with the Holy Ghost Fathers, was the first body of its kind to consecrate itself entirely to the welfare of the world's most abandoned and despised people, the Black Races of Africa. Don Bosco's Sisters, the Daughters of our Lady Help of Christians, have more than thirty houses in Africa and Asia alone. The Mill Hill Fathers have the Franciscan Missionaries of St. Joseph; and so on with the others. The *Catholic Directory* reveals the fact that a surprisingly large number of these Missionary Sisters now have foundations in this country; there are more than a dozen of them in the Southwark diocese, and nearly as many in the Archdiocese of Westminster. Nor must it be overlooked that many Religious Orders of women, including contemplatives—although not founded specifically for foreign missionary work—have established themselves in heathen territories. In a numerically small Catholic country like Holland, no fewer than thirty-five different Religious Orders of women undertake foreign missionary work; but, of course, a good proportion of these are missionary Orders.

In 1949, the Missionary Sisters of our Lady of the Rosary celebrated the silver jubilee of their establishment. This Congregation is part of the generous contribution made to the cause, in our century, by the people of Ireland. Founded, in 1924, by Bishop Shanahan of Nigeria, with its headquarters at Killeshandra in County Cavan, this Institute is now one of the leading teaching bodies in West Africa, and has been opening a new school or hospital almost annually since it moved out there. From Nigeria it went southwards to the Transvaal, and then westwards to Sierra Leone, described as one of the most difficult missions in the world. To quote from the jubilee souvenir called *Silver Sheaves*:

"The great Lion Mountains (Sierra Leone), which shadow Freetown, seem to symbolize the darker shadow which lies over the history of this region. What scenes of sorrow and terror have not these mountains witnessed! In the sheltered harbour below, many and many a slave-raider has anchored during the dark and evil years of the West African slave-trade,

when as many as 100,000 slaves were taken annually
from the coast to be sold across the Atlantic. When the
dreadful traffic was being crushed, it was in the shadow of the
Sierra Leone mountains that territory was acquired for the
liberated slaves—hence the name of Freetown. It is said that,
between the years 1820 and 1860, over 50,000 ex-slaves, all
originally from other parts of Africa, were planted around
Freetown to settle down and colonize it. No wonder a veil
of sorrow and pain hangs like a mist over the history of this
place. The many graves of missionaries—Holy Ghost Fathers
and Brothers, and the valiant Sisters of St. Joseph of Cluny—
who died here at very early ages, witness all too well to the
toll of lives demanded of them by this colony in its beginnings."

But, here again, this story multiplied a hundred times over
would hardly provide a fair picture of what has been going on
during the past three quarters of a century. The result is
that, whereas there were less than twenty thousand nuns on
the missions in 1907, there are now between sixty and seventy
thousand, inclusive of native Sisters. It is regrettable that
it is not possible to traverse the history, review the activities,
or even mention the names of the hundreds of Religious
bodies to which they belong. Did this inadequate volume
stand in need of a dedication, it might in justice be dedicated
to them; or, better still, to all the Unknown Warriors of both
sexes, to the heroic if inglorious Band of the Anonymous
and Unrecorded.

Needless to say, once they were properly settled in foreign
parts, these women applied themselves to the task of fostering
vocations among the natives. At first, this was looked upon as
a daring experiment; but, daring or not, it met with such
success that, by 1949, their numbers had increased to over
twenty-one thousand. In certain places native women may be
difficult to recruit or to train; but, given the requisite education
and spiritual formation, it is easy to see the advantages they
must possess over their European sisters. The Helpers of the
Holy Souls, for instance, arrived in China in 1867, eleven
years after their foundation by Mère Marie de la Providence.
From the very beginning they made it a point of welcoming
native women into their ranks. In 1936 they had more than a

hundred of them in their five convents in China. One of these made a great name for herself among her countrymen, who nicknamed her H'ou-Zah-Mou-Mou, that is to say "The Torch Bearer." Her career is portrayed for us in that fascinating volume *Some Sisters of Mine* written by René Bazin's daughter, herself one of the Helpers.

Coming from a good Chinese Christian family, Mother Miki (H'ou-Zah-Mou-Mou) had as a child to submit to the torture of having her feet maimed. Her shoes were taken off, her toes bent under her soles and kept in position by tight bandages. Her social standing made this necessary. The Helpers opened their first house in Kiang-Nang, and the future Mother Miki found herself one of a great number of Chinese pupils who welcomed the two first missionaries. In 1874 Catherine entered the novitiate of the order and received the name of the Japanese martyr—Saint Paul Miki. God granted her thirty-three years of apostleship.

Having some knowledge of the medicines of her country, she had made for herself the reputation of an extremely clever and capable doctor. And, indeed, her remedies were always efficacious: powders or medicine mixed in sweetened waters for infants who were seriously ailing, and the 'panacea of the sponge', otherwise Baptism, for those dangerously ill. Her funeral was attended by a great number of Chinese, to whom a request had been made that there should be none of the usual cries and demonstrations, as Mother Miki was a nun. This request all respected until the cemetery was reached. There two poor old Chinese women "could not restrain their grief, and burst into tears and lamentations. It was China weeping for H'ou-Zah-Mou-Mou."

We have the testimony of the White Fathers that, in Africa, it is easier to recruit native nuns than native lay-brothers. Archbishop Streicher, we are told, while vicar-apostolic of Uganda, "sponsored the first careful steps in this direction, and in 1919 the first nuns native to Africa, eleven Baganda women, made their simple vows. They had been trained under the White Sisters, and since then they have become an independent diocesan congregation, with their own Mother-General and a rule approved by the Holy See. They are called the Daughters of Mary (in Luanda,

12

Hannabikira) and there are over 800 of them. The principal work of these Sisters is the religious instruction of young children, but they take part in all the activities of the White Sisters; and some of them have already gained teacher's certificates, with distinction, from government education departments."

From the beginning, the Missionary Sister justified all the hopes of the optimists and belied all the misgivings of the pessimists; in nothing more so, perhaps, than in the ease with which she fitted into the missionary framework, no matter how abnormal that framework chanced to be.

One of the Missionary Sisters of the Holy Ghost, who work in conjunction with the Holy Ghost Fathers, has some good things to say concerning the ingredients that go to the making of this special vocation:

"The qualifications necessary to become a Missionary Sister are few, and not beyond the strength of any generous soul. Certainly the girl who offers herself for the Missions must give herself entirely to God and, once and for all, make the complete sacrifice of her life. But thereafter she has nothing to fear. Her superiors are too prudent to place her in a position where her material or spiritual welfare is in jeopardy. Science and research have made life in the tropics today perfectly endurable to those who will take the necessary precautions. There are even natures who can stand it better than European climates. Let it be well understood: the missionary vocation is *not* based on a love of travel or adventure. From the beginning to the end its *leit motif* is the love of God."

It was a great day for these devoted women when one of their own sex was formally proclaimed patron and protector of the Missions everywhere. St. Teresa of Lisieux had always yearned to be a missionary. Although her body remained shut up in the Carmel, her soul traversed the distant territories where so many of her countrymen were wrestling with the problems of the apostolate. In her last illness she was advised to take a turn or two in the convent garden. She was hardly able to drag herself along, but she said to one of the nuns: "Do you know what gives me strength? I offer each step for some missionary, thinking that somewhere, far away, one of them is worn out by his labours; and, to lessen his fatigue, I offer mine to God." After her death, a phenomenal devotion to her grew up in Africa, India, China and elsewhere. As the English edition of her autobiography says: "From Morocco to Natal, from Dahomey to Abyssinia, the 'White Virgin of France' was revered and loved. In Uganda a great hospital was dedicated to her. In Africa alone, seventy-one churches, thirty-seven missions, twelve seminaries and countless Congregations of Sisters, hospitals and leper homes have been dedicated to the Saint. In India and China the churches dedicated to her number one hundred and seventeen. It would be difficult to find a mission where she is not loved. In China, six vicariates, seven missions and six Congregations are placed under her protection. She is loved from the torrid regions of the Equator to the frozen ice-fields of the north where the Eskimos hold her in special veneration." This universal and unprecedented cult induced Pope Pius XI to make over the work of the apostolate in foreign lands to her intercession.

XXVI

THE CONTEMPORARY SCENE

OUR own century is, so far, conspicuous, not so much for any spectacular advance made in this or that missionary territory as for the practical measures taken with a view to future development. Two of these are of such far-reaching importance that a separate section will be devoted to each. Advances there have been, especially in Africa, but these have been neutralized by the calamities that have fallen upon the flourishing communities of China; not to speak of what has happened and is happening in Poland, Czechoslovakia, Rumania, Bulgaria, Hungary, Eastern Germany and Russia itself. When the tide of oppression in these areas has spent itself, a new missionary crusade will be called for similar to that which performed such miracles of reconstruction in the nineteenth century.

In 1922, Pope Pius XI transferred the headquarters of the Association for the Propagation of the Faith to Rome. Three years later a missionary exhibition was held in the Eternal City, during the reign of the same Pontiff whose wise policies and stirring exhortations earned for him the title of Pope of the Missions. This exhibition has now become a permanent thing with the exhibits lodged in the Lateran Palace. For the first time in history, missionaries at the ends of the earth were able to hear the voice of the Father of Christendom prompt to utilize the resources of science for the furtherance of God's Kingdom.

In England, a novitiate for the training of Sisters for the Uganda mission was opened by Mother Kevin; a Catholic Women's Missionary League was founded by Mrs. Thomas with the object of providing material necessities for the missions, such as altar furniture and school and hospital equipment; and the hierarchy appointed the second last Sunday of October, Mission Sunday, as a day on which special prayers and sermons were to be devoted to the cause.

At the beginning of this period the state-of-affairs in Africa and Asia was, roughly, as follows:—

	Converts	Missionaries	Churches	Schools
Japan	150,000	800	291	113
China	1,500,000	5,500	6,025	4,821
Further India	1,072,000	5,200	4,475	3,138
East India	58,000	520	76	96
India and				
Ceylon	2,300,000	8,000	4,980	3,636
Lower Asia	630,000	8,200	1,769	1,090
Mindanao	158,000	49	176	153

This gives a total for all Asia of nearly six million converts including Catechumens, with over twenty-seven thousand missionaries of whom some twelve thousand were nuns. The native clergy mustered considerably more than five thousand.

	Converts	Missionaries	Churches	Schools
South Africa	96,000	2,500	269	299
Central ,,	500,000	1,200	1,384	1,210
N.W. ,,	90,000	870	228	337
N.E. ,,	145,000	1,830	230	191
The Islands	560,000	740	1,307	1,355

For Africa, therefore, there was a grand total of over a million converts, and over seven thousand missionaries, about half of whom were nuns. The statistics for Australia and Oceania give one hundred and seventy thousand as the number of converts, and these were being served by about twelve hundred missionaries.

The exclusion of North and South America from this list would seem to warrant the conclusion that there are no old-time pagans left to convert in these territories. There are some, no doubt, but there are not a great number. Organized missionary work among the Eskimos was taken in hand in the year 1912, and it would be difficult, probably, to find a Redskin today who has not come under the influence of some Christian body, whether Catholic or Non-Catholic; and the same may be said, with a wider reservation, of the natives of South America. There are, however, fourteen million negroes in the United States the majority of whom have no religion of any kind. Four hundred and fifteen thousand of them are

Catholics, and this number is steadily increasing from year to year.

One final table will bring the statistics of conversions up to the latest available date.

ASIA	June 30th, 1923	June 30th, 1948
Japan	90,000	130,000
China	2,251,000	3,250,000
Korea	97,000	178,000
Indo-China, Burma ⎫ Siam, Malaya ⎭	1,340,000	1,798,000
India	2,530,000	4,668,000
Ceylon	377,000	532,000
Indonesia	143,000	732,000
Philippines	53,000	281,000
Totals	6,881,000	11,569,000
Islands East of Australia	243,000	370,000
Africa		
British Territories	725,000	3,555,000
French Territories	800,000	2,511,000
Belgian Congo	425,000	3,281,000
South Africa	220,000	741,000
Spanish Territories	61,000	218,000
Totals	2,474,000	10,676,000

According to information forthcoming in 1950, there are now in the foreign missions, strictly so called, something like twenty-seven thousand priests, of whom eleven thousand are natives; ten thousand lay-brothers, of whom about one-half are natives; sixty-two thousand nuns, of whom thirty-eight thousand are natives; and, finally, close upon one hundred thousand catechists.

It would serve no useful purpose to institute comparisons between one country and another. Still, the fact remains that the Church, in our day, is compelled—for obvious reasons—to look for support beyond the frontiers of those Catholic countries which, in days gone by, poured such abundant treasures of men and materials into the apostolate. After all, nations are like individual human beings; they reach the peak of their vigour, exhaust themselves and, then, have to lie still for awhile until their strength is built up again. Apart from that, political developments tend to push this or that people to the front in given periods, and tend equally to curtail their activities when the pendulum swings the other way. We know only too well how missionaries are apt to fare when the countries to which they belong are involved in a losing war. Into the bargain, there is the shortage of priests, an acute shortage in the case of a country like France whose response to the call was formerly so outstanding. That that response, considering everything, is still a generous one appears from the latest statistics of the personnel of the White Fathers, in which French nationals figure at the head of the list.

At the moment, Holland contains about three and a half million Catholics. Yet this plucky body manages to support some eighty-one Congregations of Religious all pledged, in whole or in part, to the training of priests, lay-brothers and Sisters for the foreign missions. In 1947, over five thousand missionaries belonging to that country were working in territories subject to the jurisdiction of Propaganda, a personnel about equal to that of Italy.

Although the Society of Bethlehem, with its headquarters at Immensee, is the only strictly missionary congregation appertaining to Switzerland, that country claims to have produced one foreign missionary for every thirteen hundred Catholics in the homeland, or thereabouts. Switzerland also excels in the production of missionary literature of high quality, and has no fewer than thirty-five magazines in circulation.

Of Canada it can now be said that there is scarcely a family in the French province that is not represented in the foreign mission fields. The old Religious Orders contribute their quota. There are, for example, sixty-one Canadian Jesuits working in China, Africa and India; twenty-two Dominicans working in Japan, India and America. The White Fathers have two hundred and eight Canadians attached to the African missions, while the Oblates of Mary Immaculate come second with one hundred and fifty-eight distributed through Africa, Indo-China and America. To these must be added one hundred and twenty-six Canadians sent out by the Foreign Mission Societies of Quebec and Scarboro respectively. These are labouring in China, San Domingo, Japan, and Indonesia. There are, besides the bodies enumerated, nearly forty other congregations of men and women which send subjects into the missions. A new English-speaking missionary community was recently founded in Ontario. When we remember that Canada was herself a missionary country not so very long ago (and indeed is still, to some extent) this must be regarded as a very creditable performance.

The same qualification covers the contribution made by the United States. The Missionary Society of Maryknoll was established in 1912, and other similar bodies have come into being since, notably the Medical Missionary Sisters, who will be referred to in a later chapter. From the *Missionary Index of Catholic Americans* published by the Students' Mission Crusade, we learn that, in 1949, 4,123 American citizens were evangelizing territories as far apart as Alaska and Argentina, Oceania and Irak—2,375 men and 1,748 women. The West Indies claimed the biggest figure, namely 716; while Oceania and China followed on with 624 and 566 respectively. Practically all the older Religious Orders are represented in this Index, the Jesuits to the amount of well over four hundred members. As might be expected, the Maryknoll Missionary body tops the list with over six hundred, men and women.

We shall allow an Irish priest, Father M. O'Carroll, to speak for his countrymen. "Irish Catholics," he writes, "were at that time (1939) providing about one-twelfth of the missionaries in territories dependent on the Congregation for the Propagation of the Faith. The official statistics for 1939 showed that, out of twenty-two thousand women working for the conversion of pagan lands, two thousand two hundred were of Irish nationality."

It was reported in the Catholic Press that five hundred priests, brothers and nuns left Ireland for the missions in 1949. The Maynooth Mission to China is composed of secular priests who have, with the approval of the Church, bound themselves by oath to labour for the conversion of the heathen. In the year 1911, an Irish priest, Rev. Edward Galvin, went to China as a missionary. In 1916 he came home determined, as he said, to bring Ireland into the Missions. In 1918, the College at Dalgan Park, in the diocese of Galway, was started with nineteen students. In two years the house was overcrowded. In 1941, 155 students took up residence in the new Dalgan Park, at St. Columban's, Navan. Branches were next established in America, Australia and New Zealand; but the college at Navan is the heart of the Society. At the moment (1949) there are in China, 104 priests of the Society working among some six and a half million pagans; in Korea, 27 priests working among four million pagans; in Burma, 32 priests working among three-quarters of a million pagans; in Japan, 16 priests working among over a million pagans. In the Philippine Islands, 68 priests are to be found in four dioceses. The total number of baptisms administered from 1920 to 1940 was 77,000. In the Philippines, in the year 1948, there were 20,327 baptisms.

The Society of St. Patrick for Foreign Missions was founded in 1932 to meet the urgent need for priests in the southeastern provinces of Nigeria in West Africa. Since then it has grown rapidly.

Of China, the present Holy Father, Pope Pius XII, declared that prosperous fields of life have been turned into cemeteries of death. At the beginning of 1950 it was reported that nearly all the thirteen thousand missionaries working in that country had been able, so far, to remain at their posts.

What makes the Soviet technique of liquidiation so effective is that, like the thumbscrew, it operates by dint of a slow but steady pressure. " The present policy", writes Father James Kearney, S.J., "is not one of physical violence towards missionaries. It is rather a war of nerves, constant and systematic vexation meant to discourage and finally exhaust the missionaries, so that they will get up and go of their own accord." Since this statement was made, there has been plenty of physical violence and even martyrdoms, as all the world knows.

The situation in Korea speaks for itself. Elsewhere in this

region, in Tibet and Indo-China, for instance, the prospects are very unpromising. Japan, however, has made a great recovery and, given a period of peace, ought to compensate in some measure for the reverses on the Asiatic mainland.

Writing in *The Tablet* in February 1950, the Right Reverend Thomas Pothacamury, Bishop of Bangalore, gives a very encouraging picture of the state of affairs in his native country.

"The faith", he says, "has taken deep roots in the soil and is not an exotic plant. Four archdioceses and eighteen dioceses are under the administration of Indian Bishops. Of 5,500 priests, over 4,000 are sons of the soil. We now have 900 students in major seminaries. There are 12,000 Religious Sisters, the great majority Indians. With the advent of independence, Christianity is no longer identified with western domination. Christians have now voluntarily surrendered the doubtful privilege of Communal electorates in the larger interests of the nation. They have played their part as citizens, and displayed more concern in the welfare of their country as a whole, than in their own political position."

The state-of-affairs in Africa, as far as statistics go, may be summarized in a few words. There are, at the present time, close upon twenty million Christians in that country, of which number considerably more than one-half are Catholic Christians. The north is still solidly Moslem, the west and Sudan less so, while there is a steady, if slow, penetration of the faith along the coast and in the region of the great lakes. The adherents of Islam are said to be about sixty million; they are still difficult to get at. It seems to be agreed that education alone will, humanly speaking, pave the way for the conversion of a people who blindly believe without ever examining the rational basis of their belief. As one missionary puts it: "When fresh air gets into a tin of corned beef, the beef becomes uneatable." And already a certain amount of fresh air is getting in. The modern social, economic and political evolution is making holes in the tin. In Egypt, Tunis and Algiers, Moslems are attending Catholic colleges, and even their women folk are beginning to realize the state of ignorance and unwholesomeness in which that system deliberately keeps them.

Prayer and example will do the rest. So at least thought

Father Charles de Foucauld, ex-soldier and explorer, who was murdered by raiders at Tamanrasset in 1917. In 1902 he established himself as a hermit in the Sahara desert where, for the next fifteen years, he lived a life of prayer and penance, always with one thought in his mind and one desire in his heart—the conversion of the Arabs. During his sojourn in the desert, de Foucauld found time to compile a Tuareg-French dictionary, and also to make a translation of the Gospels into Tuareg. His idea was to establish in this mission field communities of Religious pledged to a life of prayer and absolute renunciation.

"For some time I have been thinking a great deal about Morocco, where there are ten million people without priest or altar, where the night of Christmas will go by without sacrifice and without prayer. Pray for Morocco. Morocco will be converted—and from that victory others will follow—by souls who are bent on making every sacrifice and who have only one desire, to glorify Jesus by following and obeying Him perfectly. Worship and contemplation prepare the way for everything. When this phase is ended will be the time to sow the teaching and preaching Orders into the furrow."

It may be recalled here that, in his encyclical on the Missions, Pope Pius XI suggested that the Contemplative Orders might make foundations in foreign missionary countries.

Of the seventy million pagan inhabitants of Africa, it is believed that before long they will be done with their ancient superstitions, and will be compelled to choose between Christianity and materialism. White civilization, while it has brought great advantages to that part of the population, has nevertheless cut the past from under their feet, or wrenched them away from their ancestral roots. This has given the social agitator his chance. In 1927, the South African bishops declared that the Church will have to face up to this new situation, or lose the African. In his account of the White Fathers, Donald Attwater speaks of the insidious effect upon the natives of "the introduction of foreign manners and customs and standards and interests, all the problems and complications that commercial expansion brings with it, the emergence of the corrupt 'town Nigger,' unjust exploitation and 'labour' troubles—and these things continue and in some respects get worse; in our own day they have produced in the Congo and northern Rhodesia the pan-African communistic 'Watch Tower' movement (imported from the United States!). In Africa, as everywhere else, facts show that capitalist-industrial commercialism inevitably provides the best breeding-ground for communist propaganda."

Meanwhile, Father A. E. Howell, himself a White Father, deals with another new problem, that of African Nationalism, which, he says, the missionary must respect by making it clear that the Church loves all nations equally, and which he must safeguard by educating the natives in true patriotism.

"It is not the aim of the Church to Europeanize the native peoples." This is a Sister Doctor of the Medical Missionaries of Mary speaking. She continues: "As grace does not destroy nature, so Christianity does not (and should not) destroy native culture. Europeanization and civilization are far from being synonymous. The dress and food, for instance, of Europeans only bring disease to the natives. The outlook of the Sister must not be influenced by the Manchester cotton market, or the canned food advertisement racket. As soon as she has left the boat which brought her to the field of labour, she must learn to adapt her ways to the ways and customs of her adopted country, so long as these do not conflict with Catholic teaching or the requirements of hygiene. Catholic missionaries must take care to avoid methods which, in the past, exposed Christians to the taunt that 'trade and the Gospel follow one another'."

XXVII

A NATIVE CLERGY AT LAST

THE normal practice of the Church in evangelizing the nations of Europe was to consolidate the work as soon as possible by creating an indigenous hierarchy. It is recorded of St. Patrick that he actually ordained and consecrated three hundred and sixty-five bishops. A tradition with such a round number attached to it may well make us cautious; but it is certain that Ireland's priesthood was, from the start, a native priesthood. A partiality for such a priesthood was part of the Celtic style. St. Patrick's favourite disciple, Benen the Psalmsinger, succeeded him in the see of Armagh, and he was the son of a native chieftain. Even in Anglo-Saxon England, where things moved more slowly, we find Theodore, the Primate, consecrating native bishops within less than a century after the landing of Augustine. The appointment of the first Englishman, Berthwald, to the see of Canterbury took place in 693. In Germany, as will be remembered, Sturmi, a converted Saxon, having been ordained by Boniface, was at once entrusted with the task of evangelizing his fellow countrymen.

When, however, European missionaries directed their energies to the evangelization of the Far East and of the New World a different policy prevailed, with consequences which have lasted down to our own day. "I would rather see you ordain one indigenous priest than baptize fifty thousand heathen," said Pope Innocent XI to a missionary from China. Previously, between 1614 and 1635, a violent persecution against the Christians broke out in Japan. Blessed Luis Sotelo of Seville, a Franciscan, was one of the victims burned at the stake. He understood clearly that, had the mission been organized on a native footing, the persecution might have been avoided, or at all events stopped. While in prison, seven months before his death, he wrote a letter to the Pope in which he urged the creation of a Japanese clergy. This he considered would free the priests, who were almost all Europeans, from the suspicion of being political agents. Then again, in times of difficulty, native priests would be able to minister to the spiritual needs of the people without giving

177

offence to the authorities. His proposals arrived too late to be adopted.

One can scarcely resist the feeling that the mentality with which many of the Europeans approached the peoples whom they subjugated stood in need of an almost radical overhaul. However this may be, nothing in this line was ever seriously attempted in their newly acquired dominions. St. Francis Xavier, whose mentality was quite exceptional, did found a college in India with this object in view; but his successor in office, while retaining the college, promptly turned the native students out of doors.

The Paris Society of Foreign Missions, founded in 1658, devoted itself to the task of making good this grave deficiency. Their first seminary for the education of such natives was the one opened at Juthia, Siam, in 1664, with pupils drawn from Cochin-China, India, Japan and Tonkin. Transferred to Pulo Penang in 1805, its martyrology contains over one hundred names. In the seventeenth century, we hear of a certain Gregory Lopez, a native Chinese, who entered the Order of Preachers and became the first of his nation to be elevated to the episcopacy. A seminary for all India was founded in Ceylon, in 1893, through the influence of Pope Leo XIII.

In the year 1858, an Italian Franciscan, Father Ludovico da Casoria, was walking in the streets of Naples, when he met two black boys accompanied by a priest. Their appearance recalled to his apostolic mind the plight of Africa and, there and then, he decided to respond to an inspiration that had suddenly come to him. He opened a school and took the two boys into it as its first pupils. Later, they were joined by a number of other black boys, so that there were sixty-four in the end. Insisting, day after day, that "Africa will be converted only by Africans," he went on with the training of these future missionaries, teaching them Latin, Italian, Arabic and French. He dressed them up in Franciscan habits, and this attracted so much attention to his enterprise, that he was able to enrol a number of lay-people in a sort of Friends-of-Africa association.

In this department also women were not behindhand. In 1889, Stephanie Bigard inaugurated at Caen a work designed to provide funds for the education of native priests everywhere.

Of this enterprise it is recorded that "it represents the first really effective step taken in modern times to provide for this urgent need." It prospered and, in 1920, its headquarters having been moved to Rome, it was officially adopted by the Holy See under the title "The Pontifical Society of St. Peter the Apostle for Native Clergy."

During the nineteenth century, courageous attempts at the formation of a native clergy were made in the mission fields themselves, one of which may be cited here with a view to the removal of the impression that the neglect of this work was always due to apathy. We have seen how Father Bataillon landed on one of the South Sea Islands in 1837. His converts were such good ones that he determined to open a junior seminary and so prepare the best of them for the priesthood. In due course, all the candidates drifted back home in order to get married. Later, he took three natives to Rome and installed them in the College of Propaganda. One died there, the second failed to persevere and the third, having been ordained and having returned to the South Seas, renounced his priesthood and became a thorn in the side of the missionaries. It was not until 1886 that these converted Polynesians could be advanced to the altar with any hope of success.

It is greatly to the credit of our generation that it really wakened up to the realization that, if the future of the missions in the Far East and in Africa was to be secured, then native hierarchies there had to be, and as speedily as possible. Public opinion had been tending in that direction for some time, but the matter was clinched by the outspoken encyclical letters of Popes Benedict XV and Pius XI. As an example, the latter solemnly consecrated six Chinese bishops in 1926, and a Japanese bishop twelve months later. At the moment of writing, the Church of God possesses a Chinese Cardinal in the person of Archbishop Tien of Pekin. The encyclicals in question stressed the advantages that must accrue to the Church through the multiplication of native vocations, advantages which the passage of years has brought home to all. We have, for example, the testimony of a European bishop working in China to the effect that one native priest employed by him had made forty thousand converts—an achievement unique, surely, at any rate since the time of Francis Xavier.

Today there are some eleven thousand native priests in the missions, while about eighteen thousand native students are studying for the priesthood.

There was a time, and not so far distant either, when the mere suggestion of creating a negro clergy and episcopate would have been laughed at. Yet the White Fathers have succeeded in creating just this sort of hierarchy in the very heart of Africa. The facts are given by Donald Attwater in a booklet from which we are able to quote by courtesy of the Catholic Truth Society. "Fifty-nine mission stations with their posts and dependencies are in the sole charge of Negro clergy. Uganda has had the glory of being the first mission in Africa to provide a Vicariate entirely staffed by African priests, and with a native bishop at its head. Masaka Vicariate, in Uganda Protectorate, was erected in 1938 and confided to the care of Bishop Joseph Kiwanuka, a native of Uganda, who is also a White Father. In this part of Africa, therefore, the White Fathers have completed their task and confided what is almost a Catholic country to the care of its own native priests. There are fifteen junior seminaries and five senior in the White Fathers' missions, and in these 1,300 more young Africans are being prepared for the priesthood."

How the native women of this territory have responded to the call of the religious life has already been told in the chapter dealing with Missionary Sisters.

Donald Attwater has this to say of the Catechists. "They are usually married men of from twenty-five to fifty years old, and the training they receive depends on the work they are to do and other circumstances. Most of them are either teaching in Mission Schools, or dispersed for general religious work among the lesser villages. There are over 10,000 of these Catechists (working under the White Fathers) and their job is a whole time one which they discharge with great devotion, seriousness and volubility; with their qualifications, many of them could earn more as clerks in government offices and so forth, but they loyally stick to their job and the small salary which is all that can be attached to it. By such means and methods the White Fathers seek to achieve the aim of their founder Cardinal Lavigerie, the conversion of Africa by Africans."

XXVIII

MEDICAL MISSIONARY SISTERS

FOLLOWING the example of Jesus Christ and in response to the powers which He conferred upon them, the first missionaries made physical healing part and parcel of their apostolic routine. It is true that these miraculous gifts were not granted to all their successors; but, even after they had lapsed, we find the dispensers and propagators of the Christian religion adhering to the idea that the diseases and infirmities of the body were well within the province of their ministrations. Quite a number of pagans owed their conversion, in the first instance, to the skill and charity of the brothers Cosmas and Damian, two eminent Arabian physicians who regarded their profession in the light of an apostolate and who, owing to the fact that they accepted no fees, were called "the money-less ones." Those writers of the early Church such as Clement of Alexandria, Lactantius and St. Isidore, whose studies embraced medicine and the laws of hygiene, related these branches of knowledge to the question of salvation and the good of souls.

The hospital may not be a Christian institution, but it is certain that the care of sick people had never been so well organized, or its benefits so widely distributed, as during the early Christian centuries. As soon as the persecutions had come to an end, we find the building of infirmaries and hospices being taken in hand in big centres like Caesarea, Rome, Ostia, Constantinople and Milan. The one which the Roman matron Fabiola built and endowed in the Eternal City in the year 400, proposed "to gather the sick in from the streets and nurse them inside." This was a notable break with a past in which medical skill and attention were practically the monopoly of the well-to-do.

St. Benedict required his subjects to cultivate medical science as an aid to their duty of exercising hospitality and, in fact, Benedictine monasteries were, in some sort, clinics from which medicine and advice were dispensed to all comers. Doubtless this social service developed gradually, but it did develop. There was not a great deal that needed to be done in those robust ages when populations had to contend mostly with famines, droughts and, occasionally, with epidemics. But, with the coming of the Middle Ages, and with the new problems they brought in their train, we have a corresponding extension and multiplication of enterprises designed to alleviate and check the progress of disease. Religious Orders of Hospitallers were started and asylums for lepers were built. At this time, it was no unusual thing to find priests acting as physicians. When, after Charlemagne, educational establishments began to cover the land, the study of medicine became part of their curriculum until, at last, there was founded at Salerno what is regarded as the oldest medical school in the West.

In all these charitable undertakings women played their part. St. Paula opened a hospital for Jews in Bethlehem, and she and her daughter nursed the sick in it. St. Jerome knew at least fifteen Christian women who were studying and practising medicine in his day. Medieval women like St. Radegund and St. Hildegard were the lady doctors of their age, just as the deaconesses of an earlier period were the forerunners of our modern district nurses.

The Franciscans and Dominicans carried with them into the New World, and placed at the service of the natives, all the social services to which Christian Europe was habituated, medicine included. In Mexico, for example, a hospital was erected within twenty years of the coming of the first missionaries; and this was the procedure followed in all the big centres where the aim ever was to cater, as far as possible, for all the needs of the growing communities. In the lifetime of Champlain, a hospital was opened in Quebec to which the Indians had free access. And short of actual hospitals, every missionary settlement—such for instance as those in California—was at once a clinic and a dispensary at which advice and assistance were to be had for the asking. And just as St. Columba tackled the cattle-plagues which afflicted the Highlands in his day, so, all the way along, missionaries were only too ready to extend to the primitive people among whom they were working the benefits of their superior knowledge and experience. Cardinal Massaia, as we saw, introduced vaccination into Abyssinia, and established medical services of various kinds.

In these latter days, too, valuable lay-organizations came into being whose objective was to promote and develop this side of the missionary apostolate. Abroad, in Bavaria, Belgium, France and Switzerland, Canada and the United States, medical missionary enterprises of various kinds have been in existence for some years.

What, however, is distinctly novel and twentieth-century is the phenomenon of bodies of religious (as apart from secular) women being specially trained as doctors, nurses, midwives and technicians with a view to furthering missionary work in distant lands. For this innovation we are indebted, from first to last, to the practical good sense and determined energy of women; and of one woman, in particular, who never lived to see the accomplishment of an aim to which she devoted herself during a long lifetime.

Too little is known of Doctor Agnes McLaren outside medical missionary circles, although she must be ranked among the giants of the apostolate. The daughter of a father who, in his own way, was the champion of unpopular causes, she was to champion them all her life, and even on her deathbed. When the time was near, she was asked if she was in pain. "No," she replied, "it is not that. And it is not that I am unwilling to die. But I keep thinking of the women of India as I saw them. They were so sick and so poor; and my plans for them have not been carried out." What she had planned was the taking up by missionary Sisters of professional medical and surgical work, midwifery and all; and she passed away without seeing the removal, in 1936, of the Church's ban on the assumption of such services by nuns.

In her day there was, in this country, an implicit ban on the assumption by women of medical duties of any kind, and Agnes had to go to Montpellier to do her studies, to Ireland to take her medical degree and to Cannes for her first practice. In 1898 she became a Catholic, after attending Catholic religious services for twenty years. At her conditional baptism she took the extra name of Xavier saying, "If I had been a man, I would have been a missionary." Then she began to collect funds for the building of a hospital in India.

Protestant missionaries had been the pioneers of organized medical services in all the chief mission countries, especially

13*

in India and China. In both these places they had numerous hospitals and dispensaries, besides medical schools for the training of native doctors and nurses. Meanwhile, in the whole of India and Africa, there was not a single Catholic medical college for either men or women, and not one school for feeble-minded or backward children. Efficient training schools for nurses and midwives were so few as to be almost negligible. The Benedictines alone in China and the Jesuits at Beirut in Syria had, before the recent war, flourishing medical colleges for Catholic men and the more advanced women students.

At the beginning of this century, one of the Mill Hill Fathers had established a small hospital for women and children in Kashmir of which the Franciscan Missionaries of Mary took charge. But, being nuns, these women were not allowed to practise medicine, surgery or midwifery. On the other hand, only a woman doctor is allowed to enter the Harem and the Zenana, or to treat the Mohammedan and Hindu woman in any way. The result was, of course, a deadlock. At the age of seventy-two, Dr. McLaren travelled to Kashmir to see for herself. The missionaries whom she interviewed were unanimous in expressing the conviction that the crying need, in these territories, was for hospital work properly carried on by religious communities of women trained in the practice of both medicine and surgery. And so Agnes journeyed to Rome to lay her cause before Pope Pius XI. Five times she returned to the charge; but an experiment of this kind could not be embarked upon without a thorough investigation, and she died thirteen years before the Holy See issued a formal decree authorizing religious communities of women to take up medical work in the full sense of the words, and in fact urging them to do so. This was a complete vindication of the instinct or inspiration which had guided Dr. McLaren for so many years.

Not long after her conversion, Dr. McLaren made the acquaintance of an Austrian lady named Anna Dengel who had much the same sort of instinct. Miss Dengel went to Cork, took her medical degree, and set out for India to begin work in a small hospital at Rawalpindi of which the Franciscan Missionaries of Mary were in charge. Later she toured the

United States, as a lecturer, in the endeavour to stir up interest in medical missionary work generally, with particular reference to the need for an association of women practitioners. Things went so well in the United States that, in 1925, Dr. Anna Dengel had made a beginning with her Society. A rule had been drawn up and a house secured near Washington; and recruits were coming in. In 1926, the first member of the community, Dr. Joanna Lyons, left for India. At last, in 1936, the Holy See made its decision, which meant that Dr. Anna Dengel's Society was given the status of a religious Congregation. Since then, it has opened a number of centres in India, complete with maternity services and a training school for native nurses. It has also established itself in New Mexico and in Georgia. The Mother House of the Medical Missionary Sisters was established in Philadelphia, in 1939, while a branch has been started in South Germany and another in Holland. The English branch is at Osterley in Middlesex.

This Society was the first community of religious women founded with the specific aim of bringing professional medical assistance to the people of missionary countries. Meanwhile, other religious communities with a similar aim have been established; the Society of Medical Missionaries of Mary in Dublin in 1937 and the Daughters of Mary, Health of the Sick, in New York. The first of these took over a hospital in Drogheda and established a novitiate and training-centre there. Sisters from other Religious Orders go there to do their course. They have already founded two centres in Southern Nigeria, and two in Tanganyika. And in the mission field itself, these bodies are now setting about the training of native medical Sisterhoods.

Meanwhile, one of the Medical Missionary Sisters gives us some facts concerning health conditions in missionary countries:

" India and Pakistan need 200,000 doctors and have only 42,000. Nurses are 7,000, number needed 778,000; trained midwives 5,000, number needed 90,000; dentists 1,000, number needed 120,000. The average expectation of life is 27 years (in England and Wales it is 60 for men and 64 for women). Half the children die under the age of ten. It is known that in China the death rate is four times that of

Western countries. One hundred and fifty million people are afflicted with trachoma, which explains why one-third of the world's blind are in China. For the 1,600,000 sick on any day, there are only 12,000 doctors and 38,000 hospital beds. To even approximate Western standards, not taking into account the much higher incidence of disease, there should be 300,000 doctors and 2,000,000 hospital beds. Africa is not only full of mysteries, but full of diseases. The average death-rate of native infants in Black Africa is generally given at 40 to 60 per cent. In some tribes it reaches as high as 80 per cent. The great majority of those who die prematurely could be saved. In Africa, malaria is everywhere, and leprosy is widespread."

This propaganda may be expected to bear abundant fruit sooner or later, especially in view of the fact that medical services in highly civilized countries might possibly reach saturation point. "Medical missions," says Doctor Anna Dengel, "are a work of *restitution* as well as of charity." And she explains what she means. "Hand in hand with the discovery and Christianization of heretofore unknown parts of the world went materialistic, selfish and often brutal exploitation of the natives and their countries by colonial powers. European and American merchants committed terrible crimes against the people of other races, utterly disregarding their God-given rights and values. How many diseases were brought to Africa, China and the South Sea Islands by the white man? Some merchants went so far as intentionally to introduce certain diseases into the countries they wished to depopulate, for example measles into certain South Sea Islands. We, as Christians who profess to be followers of Him who came to make restitution to His divine Father for the sins of mankind, have a sacred duty to make up for this guilt; and the medical apostolate is one of the most fitting ways of doing it."

Pope Pius XI insisted that this work was to be undertaken, not as a mere bait, but as an obligation of charity. "The people must never get the idea that conversion and baptism are necessary to reward your devoted care. Use all the means at your disposal to make them experience in their own bodies that your religion is good, excellent and desirable, that it is truly inspired by self-sacrificing love."

XXIX

EPILOGUE

THE first Christian Missionary might have done a number of things. He might have evangelized the whole world in person. Failing that, He might have raised up a host of Apostles of the calibre of St. Paul, and intensified their miraculous powers to such a degree as almost to compel conviction. He might have interfered with the course of history so far as to have stayed the hand of the persecutor, stifled the discordant voices of the heretics and allowed Mahomet to die in his cradle. He might have seen to it that the New World was discovered in the thirteenth century, say, when the affairs and mentality of Christendom were in better shape. At any rate, He might have assigned the colonial expansions of the fifteenth and sixteenth centuries to others besides the Portuguese and Spaniards. He might have averted the blow that fell upon the Jesuits, and the blow that fell upon Europe at the French Revolution. He might have—but, in fact, there is no end at all to the might-have-dones and might-have-beens.

As it was, our Saviour's personal ministry lasted for about three years and was restricted to the narrowest possible area. How many were privileged to hear the words of salvation uttered by His sacred lips can never be known—perhaps twenty thousand at most. The largest audience He ever had at one time amounted to a fourth part of that number. And, as though to emphasize the point that the value of missionary work is not always to be estimated in terms of immediate conversions, He Himself had few actual converts to show. The germs of the Word were, no doubt, implanted in many hearts, but they did not reach maturity in His lifetime.

For the perpetuation of His apostolate, He chose the men of His time and place; and men, by nature, humdrum and ordinary men. And these, like Himself, were to effect but little in their own brief day. What the Twelve lived to see was insignificant in comparison with the triumphs witnessed by their successors. Clearly, He willed the fabric of His kingdom to go up brick by brick and layer by layer, by means of a patient and permanent building operation, and one liable to

the interruptions, hindrances, defects and subsidences of
building operations generally.

Then, too, just as He was subjected, in His human nature,
to the vicissitudes of the temporal, so was it to be with His
Mystical Body; His Church has no option but to live and
develop in the midst of secular society, sharing its ups and
downs, being warmed and cooled by its summer and winter,
experiencing its smiles and its frowns, and being conditioned,
to some extent, by its outlook and its conceptions. St. Teresa
of Avila wondered why God allows the path of His representatives to be beset by such obstacles and difficulties. Why, indeed,
if it be not that access to the kingdom is by way of "many
tribulations", as the Scripture says.

Fortunately, the Church is not given to brooding or sulking
over the mistakes and misfortunes of the past. As soon as may
be, she is back at the scene of the disaster, concerned with the
wreckage only with a view to an immediate reconstruction.
From age to age, she can be seen returning and returning to
the charge, refusing to acknowledge defeat and maintaining
her mission with baffling persistency. Cut down a hundred
times over, the ancient stem insists on putting forth new shoots.
True to the pattern set within the first years of the apostolate,
the wind of persecution blows the seed out of one field into
another. And, thus, the work goes on, and will go on until the
fashion of this world has passed away forever.

The complaint of yesterday and today will be the complaint
of tomorrow; of all the tomorrows, since it is a divinely-
consecrated complaint: "The Harvest is great but the
Labourers are few". At the Vatican Missionary exhibition
there was a chart showing the relative proportion of converted
and unconverted in our time. The number of Jews was given
as thirteen million, of Mohammedans as two hundred and
forty million, and of heathen as one thousand million more or
less. The figures were represented by small squares each
signifying a million people. In the middle of this block of
squares was a red square standing for the one hundred and
twenty-five thousand missionaries working in heathen
lands. The caption underneath read "David facing
Goliath."

The permanent miracle of the apostolate is just that—the

relative size of the antagonists. Twelve men had to face the Goliath of the Roman Empire, and not the least remarkable thing about St. Paul is that there was only one of him. In the sub-apostolic age one looks in vain for bands of missionaries; the oft-recurring story ever is of two's and three's, of such and such a bishop or disciple or slave setting the ball rolling. St. Patrick was almost, if not quite, single handed; and so were Ninian and Kentigern and Aidan. Columba began with a dozen helpers at most. No *band* makes its appearance until St. Augustine's time, and his amounted to about forty all told. "The conversion of the heathen," writes Newman, "is ascribed to champions of the faith so few in number that we may almost count them."

It was not army-corps or divisions that marched to the spiritual conquest of Europe but a succession of mere platoons; while the New World was evangelized by quite small groups of missionaries. One's mental picture of St. Francis Xavier is that of a lonely and isolated figure standing out against the almost limitless background of the Far East. The records even of the nineteenth century, for all its teeming energy. abound in pictures of the same identical kind. That admirable book, *The Workers are Few*, has a chapter entitled "Invitations from across the Sea", in which examples are given of the kind of letters missionaries have been sending home for hundreds of years. One and all testify to the grief and sorrow of those compelled to look on, while an over-ripe harvest is decaying for want of hands to gather it in.

"It is", says Newman again, "the keen vision, the intense conviction, the indomitable resolve of the *few* that is the instrument of heaven."

Still, it would be unfortunate if this truth were to be turned into an excuse for ignoring the call of the Master. "Should the grace of God inspire within you a desire for this work, do not trample it under foot. If God tells you to leave your native land, make haste to depart, because souls are in readiness and, in you, await their Saviour. Turn your steps towards those Institutions and Religious Societies to whom the Holy See has committed the task of tilling the fields of the Church . . . The fish are abundant but the fishermen are not able to draw all into their nets. Who will go forth? O Lord, say to a large number of volunteers: Come after me and I will make you to become fishers of men."

Send forth Thy Spirit and they shall be created
And Thou shalt renew the face of the earth.

APPENDIX

THE following table shows the position in eastern and southern Asia, and in Africa as a whole, according to the latest statistics issued by the Congregation of Propaganda. It is in these two continents that the Christian religion has made least progress.

ASIA			Inhabitants	Catholics	Priests
India & Pakistan	..	..	408,000,000	4,741,000	5,605
Ceylon ..	..	..	7,270,000	538,000	423
Burma ..	..	..	18,500,000	131,000	225
Malacca..	..	..	5,800,000	93,000	69
Siam ..	..	..	18,000,000	53,000	120
Cambodia	..	..	3,100,000	110,000	106
Laos ..	..	..	1,100,000	32,000	60
Vietnam	..	..	21,000,000	1,381,000	1,766
China ..	..	..	465,000,000	3,266,000	2,602
Korea ..	..	..	28,700,000	182,000	252
Japan ..	..	..	82,500,000	131,000	595
Indonesia	..	..	26,800,000	780,000	664
Brit. Borneo	..	..	1,000,000	24,000	53
New Guinea	..	..	—	85,000	137
Totals ..	..		1,086,770,000	11,547,000	12,677

AFRICA			Inhabitants	Catholics	Priests
North East	..	..	67,400,000	2,681,400	2,011
West ..	..	..	50,990,000	1,506,800	1,299
Central	..	..	21,775,000	4,456,000	2,477
South ..	..	..	26,135,000	2,048,000	1,592
East ..	..	..	16,440,000	2,289,000	1,471
The Islands	..	..	5,052,000	1,114,000	552
Totals ..	..	..	187,792,000	14,095,200	9,402

The next table shows the position in the territories subject to Propaganda; that is to say, in what are called Missionary Countries. These include, over and above the ones mentioned in the previous table, Australia, New Zealand and Oceania; Arabia, the Balkan States (from which the available statistics

are negligible), as well as Scandinavia, Finland, Iceland and
Gibraltar; and, finally, Central and South America, parts of
Canada, and Alaska.

Catholics	27,944,894
Under Instruction	2,540,883
Priests	26,840
Brothers	9,331
Sisters	61,577
Catechists	82,863
Lay Teachers	92,111
Students in Seminaries	15,695
Schools	47,730
Pupils	4,101,654
Dispensaries	3,132
Hospitals	1,115
Leper Hospitals	174
Orphanages	1,720

INDEX